No, I'm Not Fine. Thank You.

No, I'm Not Fine. Thank You.

My Relentless Journey
To Healing Complex Trauma

Laura Renner

For more information, email noimnotfinethankyou@gmail.com.

ISBN: 979-8-88759-791-1 (paperback)
ISBN: 979-8-88759-890-1 (hardcover)
ISBN: 979-8-88759-792-8 (ebook)

Want some resources for trauma healing? Get your free copy of my ultimate list of podcasts, YouTube channels, courses, and therapy modalities to heal from trauma. This is a must-have resource for anyone looking to start or continue their trauma healing journey. Go to https://www.laurarenner.me to get your copy today.

Contents

Part 4: Game-Changing Shifts Within Myself

Part 1

Here's What Started it All

Chapter 1

The Introduction to Laura Renner

No moment in my life has been as scary as reading the results of my brain scan after my accident and seeing the words "multicompartmental acute intracranial hemorrhage." I felt every cell in my body pause as I frantically reread that sentence in my medical chart. What did this mean?

Well, nothing good. There were hemorrhages (internal bleeding) at three levels inside my skull and a large hematoma (a pool of clotted blood) at another level. And these bleeds were pressing onto my brain and forcing it downward toward my brainstem until I'd inevitably stop breathing. Oh, and a skull fracture, of course. My heart rate was through the roof. There was nothing positive in the radiology note. I said to my boyfriend, Andrew, in sheer terror, "This is really bad. Like, I might die." And then the tears shot out of my eyes like a geyser. *Oh my god, oh my god, oh my god*, kept racing through my injured brain as panic took over.

They really shouldn't let you access medical results on your own. Working as a charge nurse in a high-level neonatal intensive care unit (NICU) taught me that, but experiencing it from the patient side was a whole different can of worms. There was also a big part of me that wanted to throw my arms in the air and yell, "Are you fucking kidding me? Again?!" This was the third December in four years where I had an accident that took a big swing at my health. A major malfunction of my body. A seemingly simple fall that caused a skull fracture and internal bleeding at multiple levels on my brain.

You may be wondering, who is this person? Hi, I'm Laura. I'm someone who almost died—multiple times, actually. I experienced years of significant emotional abuse, traumatic accidents, and a slew of other not-so-stellar events. Luckily, I'm also an oversharer, which can serve as a benefit when helping others.

Have you ever noticed whenever someone is really not okay, you ask how they're doing and they often respond with, "I'm fine"? Oh boy, that is me to my very core. My response was always, "I'm fine." But I was never fine. I was in a constant state of hovering around a barely functional baseline, but to me that was normal. I didn't want to discuss the chaos swirling beneath the surface for fear of crying or having a panic attack. And I didn't want to burden other people with my problems. So I was "fine."

Then the brain scan happened. This is where the hard stop to my life as I knew it and the abrupt jump into deep trauma healing began. I took a complete 180 and gave myself no other choice. I realized I kept saying, "Fuck my life," and not, "Fuck this shit." I always expected bad things to happen to me because a lot of bad things *did* happen to me. The odds were never in my favor, hence the "fuck my life." Then I had an epiphany and decided to take control and separate the problems from my identity. So I said, "Fuck this shit," to the problems. Once I did, that lit a fire under me to make some heavy changes. So this has been my year of healing exploration, reaching depths of healing I never recognized were, A, a problem or, B, remotely plausible. This is my commitment to myself that I'm worth it. I'm over just getting through it. I want to live and enjoy the hell out of my life.

This book is one of those changes. This is my story of being resilient as hell and the shifts that enabled me to climb my way out of the trenches. Now, this isn't your "typical" trauma story. A lot of books about trauma are dense, often packed to the brim with information that can read like a textbook. Many are written by therapists who talk about their patients' struggles with some really heavy stuff, such as severe neglect, repeated rape, and daily violence from a parent. These devastating events occurred for years and would be vividly described, which were hard for me to digest. That was my bar for what trauma meant. Anything at or above those levels equaled trauma, and anything below didn't. In fact, until recently I didn't characterize a lot of the events I describe in this book as trauma at all. When I heard the word trauma I exclusively thought of things like losing a limb in war, your house catching on fire, a sudden tragic loss of your child, et cetera. But trauma doesn't need to be that extreme to hurt you. It took me thirty-four years to realize, *Oh shit, I have experienced a lot of trauma in my life.* Truthfully I thought I lived a normal pattern of life's ups and downs. For the bad stuff, I told myself I had particularly bad luck. I would joke that I must have been a high-ranking Nazi in a past life because bad things just kept shooting my way. It wasn't until I started healing that I began accepting the things that happened to me.

The last five years have been very challenging for me—lots of health problems for a seemingly healthy person in their early thirties. I broke six bones, developed a blood clot in my lung, and had a seizure, just to name a few. But it took a traumatic brain injury that almost killed me at the end of 2021 to wake me up to the stark reality that I needed to make some big changes. Through my healing process, I became fascinated by complex trauma's implications on my own health. I've done a ton of research to figure out what was wrong with me and how to get better. And I started writing as a means of processing all the bullshit.

I'm not sugar-coating anything here. I'm being incredibly vulnerable, which was previously my biggest fear. But now I fear that this could be happening to someone else who hasn't had their wake-up call. That's why this is meant to be relatable. I'm providing you with my unique perspective on the craziness that transpired in my own life and all of the healing modalities I've sampled. And despite a lot of bad odds, I've made it through some seriously dark times. This is meant to show you that we've all been through tough situations and are capable of healing.

Please be forewarned: this book is packed with a lot of trauma and may be triggering. So if you need to step away from time to time or skip around, I completely understand. Don't let the sarcasm and profanity fool you, though. I'm very serious about trauma healing. Also keep in mind, I am not a licensed therapist. I'm someone who devoted the last year of their life to healing, and this is my experience. So fasten your seat belt, and let's get this ride started.

Chapter 2

Why Trauma is so Important

I have had over three decades of consistent trauma exposure starting at age three. Early years of my life had multiple trajectory-changing events. A near-death experience, multiple injuries, and violations to my body kept me in a persistent state of fear. Later, I worked as a neonatal intensive care unit nurse, which was chock-full of daily traumas. I experienced many unexplained, bizarre health problems. My relationships were boiling over with toxicity—one event, after another, after another—sudden acute traumas and slow-burn chronic traumas. I felt like I was running on a hamster wheel of never-ending bad things. What sucks the most is I'm far from alone here. In fact, the majority of us humans have lived trauma-heavy lives. Some have experienced truly colossal levels of trauma, but in reality, we all have experiences that have dipped our toes in the trauma pool. This taught me that, in a way, trauma is important because of how universal an experience it is.

Life is filled with challenging things that happen to us, impacting our world view and our view of ourselves.

There is a disgusting amount of bad shit happening all the time, and collectively we are recognizing how much this wires our bodies and minds. There is extensive research into developmental trauma, post-traumatic stress disorder (PTSD), physical abuse, and many other types of trauma and how they manifest into physical, emotional, and brain chemical changes. Statistically 60 percent of men and 50 percent of women have experienced a traumatic event in their lifetime. I'd argue it's 100 percent. We've all experienced something so bad it stuck with us and shaped how we think, altered how we act, and changed the path of our lives in some form.

That's why identifying trauma is extremely helpful. As a recovering objective, only-trusting-in-logic kind of gal, I needed statistics attached to facts to make them real. This is dumb for numerous reasons, but especially when discussing trauma. Trauma is annoyingly unquantifiable. There's no trauma scale that perfectly captures the severity that a traumatic event impacts someone. Many people don't realize they're experiencing symptoms related to trauma, yet they can be deeply affected by them. We can identify trauma as a number of things, but it all boils down to something that has a damaging effect on your psyche.

Here we can bring in some logical systems, thankfully. One way trauma is categorized is by splitting it into "Big T" and "little t" trauma. When most of us think about trauma, we think of the Big Ts. These are the life-threatening and completely uprooting life events—sexual assault, natural disasters, physical attacks, domestic violence, and other serious events that change the course of your life. Little ts are considered personal highly distressing events such as divorce, emotional abuse, and bullying. These events can happen frequently without changing much about your daily life, which makes many people falsely assume they're not traumatic.

Even with this system, it's hard to clearly outline what trauma is. This is because it's highly individualized regarding interpretation. It doesn't matter if it's generally defined trauma—if it fucks you up, it's trauma. When I was little, I was at a gardening store with my mom and sister, Amy, and I was admiring this terracotta bunny. I picked it up, almost immediately dropped it, and the tail snapped off. My mom was not pleased and said she now had to buy it since I broke it. She explained on the way home that we don't touch things in stores because that's what happens. I felt ashamed and couldn't look at the bunny without feeling guilt. The intensity of the guilt lessened over time since my mom put the broken bunny in our backyard. I saw it daily through the back windows of our house for almost twenty years. She didn't intentionally do it to punish me, but that memory constantly lingered in my mind. Suffice it to say that messed me up on some level as a frequent reminder that I made a mistake, even though I did it as a child. So yeah, trauma can be anything painful that impacts you, but hopefully not involving more harm to terracotta bunnies. Those at least can be thrown away.

Trauma's origin may be ambiguous, but its effects are not. The more levels of chronic or acute trauma you experience, the more likely you are to be affected by PTSD or biochemical changes in the brain. It's wild how much trauma screws with our brains. When I underwent brain mapping (also known as a quantitative electroencephalogram) to determine my brain's unique electrical pattern to help treat my anxiety, sleep concerns, and heal from my traumatic brain injury, the therapist expressed multiple times how much trauma significantly impacted my brain—and not just physical trauma.

Here's some general information on areas of the brain that are affected by significant stress, so you can understand how they're affected (and because your girl here loves science). The three areas of the brain that are significantly impacted by PTSD are the prefrontal cortex, amygdala, and hippocampus. The prefrontal cortex is located in the frontal lobe and manages all things emotions, whether it's regulating, interpreting, or suppressing them. The prefrontal cortex also handles memory storage and elimination, decision-making, sleep regulation, and numerous other vital functions. The amygdala is small, but mighty. It attaches significance to emotional memories and identifies threats for survival purposes. The amygdala is your go-to for the fight or flight (acute stress) response. This is your body's internal fire alarm, which is, unsurprisingly, triggered almost immediately in many traumatic events. The hippocampus plays a major role in learning and also decides what short-term memories make the cut to become long-term memories.

That's when everything's working as intended, but the consequences of traumatic stress on the brain change that. The prefrontal cortex, amygdala, and hippocampus basically get thrown into an ice-cold pool. They try to keep swimming around to warm up, but the stress of being in the cold pool negatively alters how they function. Once they make it out of the pool, they're drenched in dysregulation and fear, and that becomes the new norm.

To make matters worse, the prefrontal cortex, amygdala, and hippocampus have crossovers in their jobs, so when it comes to traumatic stress, they all go slightly more haywire together. When your amygdala is dysregulated, it inappropriately sounds the fire alarm of fight or flight, causing your prefrontal cortex to say, "Hang on, is this for real?" But because these perceived threats happen so frequently, your prefrontal cortex loses its skill at identifying what's truly a threat and what isn't. This is like when you hear a loud noise and freak out because you think it's a gunshot, only to find it was a car engine backfire. In essence, these areas of your brain become hypervigilant and overly aroused, so even small things set off all the alarm bells. Let's not forget about our friend the hippocampus. This one also goes into a tailspin and either leads to recurrent memories or dissociation, and it atrophies, or wastes away. It actually shrinks in size due to decreased activity and function—the wonders of the human body.

But, hey, anatomy helps us understand ourselves better, and my goal is to normalize trauma in a you-are-not-alone way. Because, let's be real, we're all in this trauma circle together. My previous iteration of myself would hear the word trauma and think shame, sympathy, and *oh, how tragic* (kind of a bitchy response). But that is ill-informed and inaccurate. We have all experienced trauma, and instead of feeling bad for someone, we should be empowering each other to heal from it. I want to scream that from the rooftops, but also I have a healthy level of embarrassment and desire to fit in with my neighbors, so we'll table that for now. But I look forward to the day we can all band together to heal as a community because, let's face it, we all (and I mean *all*) have healing to do. Once we normalize trauma and see it in each other as well as ourselves, we can get there.

Chapter 3

December 2017: The First of Multiple Bad Decembers

No, this isn't about me hating the holidays. Relax. Remember earlier when I mentioned this was the third December in four years that something bad happened to me? Yeah, that's our next stop on the Trauma Express— all aboard. Technically this was November 29, 2017; however, it wasn't until December where it got interesting. November 2017, I was living what I thought was my best life. I was twenty-nine. My divorce finalized a few months prior. I was dating for the first time in almost a decade. I was doing all kinds of things by myself for the first time and absolutely loving it. One of those things was snowboarding. I live in Colorado, so it's a right of passage to at least attempt to ski or snowboard. My favorite mountain (and frankly only mountain) I snowboarded was Arapahoe Basin. The beauty of being a nurse was I could go during weekdays and beat the rush of humans, which is my goal in most areas of life. Since I was new and therefore bad at snowboarding, this was great for me.

I headed up early (for someone who worked night shifts) on a Wednesday to snowboard by myself. It was my last run of the day. I was making my way down an offshoot of a run through the trees. It was beautiful. I was picking up more speed than I ever had before, but was going with it because I was a pro now, obviously. I finally felt like I had picked it up.

And then I caught an edge and immediately went down hard. It happened at what felt like lightning speed, and I felt this horrifically sharp pain radiate from the top of my hip. It knocked the wind right out of me. I rocked back and forth on the ground in an enormous amount of pain, gasping for air. I sat there wincing in pain, waiting for someone to come by to get help for me. But no one came. I sat for ten minutes and not a single person came by. And guess what? There was less than an hour until the lift closed. I realized I was going to have to board down the rest of the way. *Fuuuck.* Keep in mind that I'm not a good snowboarder and I'm prone to falling. Now I had to get down while buckled over in pain, hoping I didn't hurt myself more. Yeah, not ideal. I slowly made my way down the mountain, and my upper hip and low back area were on fire. As I reached the bottom I thought, *What are they going to do for me here?* I decided it was best to get home and see if it improved. Cue the buzzer—wrong answer, Laura.

I waddled over to my car, attempting to see if there was any bizarre gait pattern that would reduce my lower back pain, but of course, there wasn't. As I sat in my CR-V waiting for it to warm up, I thought for a second, *Can I do this right now?* and immediately followed that thought with, *Guess I kind of have to, so let's go.* I kept adjusting my position in the seat, begging for mercy. Move the seat forward a bit? Worse. Bring the incline back? Zaps down the lower half of my body. Nothing worked, but I kept at it thinking it had to get better. I even pulled over a few times to stand and see if that would reduce the piercing pain through the lower half of my back, but no. You'd think by now I'd say, "Hold on, Laura, something may be really wrong here." But here are some important facts about 2017 Laura Renner—I was stubborn, I never believed things were as bad as they were as a coping mechanism, and I was incapable of asking for help. So I kept on the sixty-four-mile drive home. As I got closer to Denver, I surrendered to the thought of getting a medical opinion. Urgent care seemed like a good fit. This wasn't an emergency by any means, but I needed to be seen to be sure it wasn't anything serious. This is where my signature move of going to urgent care over the hospital first began.

I was a bit of a shitshow in the lobby of the urgent care. I was in so much pain that I couldn't sit, I couldn't stand, and I couldn't walk well, so I did a culmination of them all at a very rapid pace, which I'm sure contributed to some degree as to why I didn't get seen quickly. Finally I heard, "Laura Renner?" As I let out a sigh of relief, my abdomen braced and a sharp pain spread up my body. The physician's assistant at urgent care was unimpressed. I wasn't in enough pain for it to be fractured, so she spared me the cost of an x-ray, which I was stoked about.

My inability to pinpoint pain is comical. I kept pointing to the right upper gluteal area of my low back thinking that was the culprit. Her consensus was that it must be a piriformis (located in the hip) muscle strain based on the manual tests she put me through. The remedy? Rest, pain medication, and it would go away with time. *What a relief,* I thought at the time. She prescribed me a few days of Percocet and scheduled me for an appointment with an orthopedist a few weeks down the road in case it didn't get better. "You can always cancel if you don't need it, but they're hard to get in to." Great. I have a plan, I have pain medication, and I can start feeling better. Turned out I would not feel better, so bless that woman for scheduling a backup plan.

The next few weeks were brutal, but partially because I was a dumbass. I continued living my life normally, which is exactly the opposite of what I should have been doing. I went to spin classes and suffered through intense pain. I got a massage and held my breath throughout the process in an effort to brace through the pain. I worked my normal shifts as a nurse, on my feet for twelve hours three times a week, even though my lower back felt like it had been run over by a car. If I could have snorted ibuprofen during this time, I would have. Instead I pushed the upper limits of the suggested oral dosing and probably the upper limits of my stomach lining as well. Still, I was struggling hard. I had coworkers plastic wrap ice packs to my midsection for hours at a time. I leaned on every available surface. Countless times I was asked if I was okay and I knee-jerk responded like clockwork,

"Oh yeah, just back pain." I assumed this was standard back pain and fully understood why it was a hundred-billion-dollar industry. Because it truly sucked.

By the time my doctor's appointment came around, I was elated. I could breathe, but only so deep before the pain clapped back at my lung expansion. The physician wasn't sold on the piriformis suggestion. She reiterated I wasn't in enough pain for it to be a fracture, especially given the location I was describing, but decided to go ahead with an x-ray just to rule everything out. Plus, they offered x-rays on site. I popped in for the x-ray, popped back out, and we looked together at the film. She had this perplexed look and pointed to my first lumbar vertebra, L1, and said, "There's a deformity there. Have you had a spine x-ray before?" Sure hadn't. She suggested an MRI (magnetic resonance imaging, which is more detailed) to explore further. Great, got that on the books. Let's see where it goes.

You would think at this point all signs pointed to something more being wrong. I was plastic wrapping ice to my back and sucking down ibuprofen like it was candy, but no, I was fine. I got the phone call from my doctor to discuss my MRI results and she immediately opened the conversation with, "You have a wedge compression fracture in your L1." *Passengers, prepare for turbulence.*

"What?"

Then she followed with, "You need to stop working immediately, and you need to be in a back brace for twelve weeks."

16

Wait, what? I could feel the space around me depressurizing. *A wedge compression fracture? That means I broke a lumbar vertebra. Wait, my back is really broken? How is this possible? I was living my best life after my divorce, and now this?!*

In tears, I called the unit where I worked saying I had a broken back and needed to cancel my upcoming shifts and crawl into a hole for the next three months. Meanwhile, my thoughts were racing. *How am I going to date with a back brace? How am I going to get groceries?* As the tears flooded down my face, I couldn't help but think my ex-husband won. I was doing so well since the divorce and now took what felt like one hundred steps backward. He got to be happy and do fun things and I had to sit at home in my goofy metal back brace and be sad. Life stopped for me. And I was crushed.

This is where my mind was in what felt like its most natural state, bullying myself. All these horrible thoughts were swirling through my brain. *How could I be so stupid? I'm such an idiot. I deserved this to happen because I'm such a piece of shit. Only bad things happen to me. I can't do anything right. I'm such an embarrassment. I'm such a bad person, and I deserve this.* As uncomfortable as these thoughts sound, they were home to me. It was how I always spoke to myself. It's how my ex-husband spoke to me. It's what I imagined people thought of me. And I took these on as core beliefs and let these thoughts go rampant through my mind.

I tried to make the best of it. I even bought tops to match my back brace. Quieting the pain was going pretty well for me until I sliced my lip open, falling face first onto concrete. That was another "are you fucking kidding me?" moment. In hindsight, I absolutely necessitated stitches, but guess who didn't go to the hospital? This gal. My already tenuous mental status sunk even lower. It was just a constant state of, "No, Laura, remember your life sucks. Stop trying to make it better because it's bad, and you need to accept that." After a few weeks my lip healed and left a scar as a reminder of that rough patch. And with time (twelve weeks, to be exact), my L1 vertebra healed, so I was able to return to work, life, and the level of normalcy I so desperately sought. I thought this was a rock-bottom moment, only to learn that would develop later.

Chapter 4

December 2018:
Another Bad December

Now, December 2018 is when things got really interesting in my life. This is when all kinds of unexplained, scary, seemingly life-threatening problems open-hand smacked me right in the face. I finally got my back situation in order, and life was going pretty well. It was December fifth, and I was working a typical night shift in the neonatal intensive care unit. I was sitting at a computer, documenting patient notes while talking to my coworker, Megan. Suddenly, I felt this extreme, unexplained sense of déjà vu and felt an overwhelming whoosh through my body indicating I was going to pass out. As Megan was talking, I gripped on to the side of the desk to make sure I wouldn't fall. It felt like the longest minute of my life where I saw stars, darkness started falling over my field of vision, my heart raced, a buzzing feeling zipped through my entire body, and then it was over. My vision returned to normal, my heart rate slowed back to its baseline, and I went back to typing away at my desk. Megan didn't notice, and I didn't say anything.

Did I pause to think that was weird? Briefly, yes. Earlier in the day, I was on a walk and had the same thing happen. I had this intense déjà vu feeling that came out of nowhere, my vision turned dark, and I felt a rush through my body. I leaned heavily onto the building next to me as the sensations took over my body. Then, it just moved through me, and I was back to normal. *That was weird*, I thought, but kept moving. Did I say something to Megan—or anyone, for that matter? No. I just moved on as if it were a normal reaction. Yeah, that was dumb. I was used to weird things happening in my body, so I brushed it off. My whole life was built around dismissing discomfort, and this was no different. I moved on and forgot about it. The remainder of my shift was uneventful. The process of getting home and going to bed was so routined I didn't log it as a unique memory. I drove home, got in bed, threw my eye mask on, and passed out.

My first memory was waking up in excruciating pain a few hours later on the morning of December sixth. I felt it all through my chest and upper back. I fought to take breaths, as every time I did my body froze from severe pain. *What is happening?* I gripped the side of my bed for dear life, then stumbled over to the bathroom mirror to see what was wrong with me. Nothing. I looked fine minus the overarching grimace that took over my face from the deafening pain. I felt like I was being stabbed from the inside out. Something was wrong.

So I did what any smart person would do at this moment. I got in my car and drove to urgent care. (Sensing a theme here?) I struggled so much to speak that I was seen immediately. The medical provider insisted on calling an ambulance to take me to the hospital. I knew how expensive ambulance rides could be and said, "No, I'll have someone drive me" (lie). He urged me not to drive and made me promise that I would leave my car and have someone pick me up. "Yes," I muttered in between the shallow breaths I was fighting to take. So I left and waddled over to my car, got in the driver's seat, and sat for a few minutes. "I can do this." *No you can't, bitch, but you're clearly going to.* As I slightly shifted my body to the right to reverse, I yelled out in pain and started crying, but it didn't stop me. I still drove myself to the hospital. (Note to readers: Do not be me. Do not make these risky decisions. Thankfully, I made it there in one piece, but I could have just as easily not, and the cost of a safe ambulance ride is always worth it.)

I would say it was a particularly busy day in the emergency department, but every day at this hospital was maximum-capacity busy, which was unfortunate for me. I got terrible care for a multitude of reasons. Too many patients and not enough staff or beds was a huge part. Still, I knew something was really wrong with me, but no idea what or why, so I wanted to give the clearest picture of my life before this afternoon.

I went for a hike the previous weekend, where I fell through the ice (yes, one fun accident after another). It sounds worse than it was; trust me. I was going through a snow-covered area close to the end of the trail, but the snow had covered the creek, and I took a casual, yet confident step straight into knee-deep water and hit hard. My adrenaline kicked into high gear, so I pulled myself out, brushed myself off, and walked out seemingly unscathed. I didn't have any pain outside of the initial smash to my foot, and after a few hours, that faded. In the days following, I worked, went to spin classes, and even did some heavy back squats with my trainer the day prior with zero pain or signs of something wrong. But the medical team clutched on to this piece of information like it was gold. They started asking me a million questions about the hike, even though I knew it was definitely unrelated.

Another fun honesty factor that I included in my medical history was how much I drink. You're "supposed" to say less than seven drinks a week for women to not be thrown into the alcohol abuse category. I told them twelve a week, which was a lowball figure, but I also didn't want to fully lie. I didn't want to ring the alarm bells of "alcoholic over here!" But I did want to give a more accurate picture of my health since I was terrified. This was another strike against me. I was treated as a drug seeker. In the hospital, a drug seeker is someone who exaggerates their pain to get pain medication (typically opiates like oxycodone). Often, their pain levels don't match their actions, such as they say they are ten out of ten on the pain scale (indicating severe pain), yet they can laugh and talk on the phone. This often leads to healthcare providers losing trust in the patient and not believing what they say.

My history and input no longer mattered. I told them how I had broken my back before and this pain was significantly worse, but I think that only added to the drug seeker profile. I received multiple eyerolls and puzzled looks from the healthcare team when I was struggling from pain to take deep breaths while they listened to my lungs. I felt like they thought I was acting. I waited as patiently as I could, but I was in such severe pain I kept calling the nurse begging for help. It seemed like they thought I was there for drugs. I had a nurse tell me to "relax" in an irritated tone when she came to give me pain medication. At one point, the attending physician came into the room and yelled at me about how I wasn't being honest about being drunk on my hike, and that's why I fell. *What the fuck?* As someone who openly loves her booze, I'm not actually an alcoholic. And why would I

1. get blasted on a hike,
2. get blasted on a hike by myself, and
3. lie about it?

I told all this to the attending and medical team, but they didn't believe me. I gave them every iota of information I could think of, but it didn't matter. They could not wait to get me discharged and free up a bed. I had to show I could walk for them to be able to send me home. I was sobbing, struggling to stand as the physical therapist watched, and begging her not to make me do this. But she told me I must. The pain was so excruciatingly gut-punching. This moment has been seared so deeply into my brain. I had never, and thankfully still to this day have never, experienced pain this severe.

At this point, my friend, Kelsey, showed up and told them she'd never seen me like this before. I could handle pain, but I could not handle this. Kelsey, also a physical therapist, reiterated how I broke my back before and it was nothing like this, so something must be wrong. But sadly, this made no impact. They still wanted to send me home. They ran a few blood tests on me, which included a drug panel that was all negative, and an x-ray.

Before leaving, I finally got the results of my x-ray from a reluctant physician who told me I had a compression fracture at T6 (meaning I broke my sixth thoracic vertebra in my spine), so they were going to keep me overnight. Wait, *what?* How is this possible? I was sleeping and just spontaneously fractured my back? I was so discombobulated. My head was spinning. I went knuckles-deep into googling spontaneous thoracic fractures.

The next morning as they hustled me out the door, I was sent home with a few Percocet and instructions to follow up with an orthopedist. That next week was the ultimate blur. I was experiencing memory loss. I was in a constant state of intense pain all through my chest and upper back. The Percocet wasn't doing anything for me. Over the next few days, I went back to the hospital twice because deep in my soul I knew there was something wrong. However, my self-reported health history and supposed alcohol abuse kept me in the drug seeker category. I was drug tested immediately with each emergency department visit. Between the frequent sighs, eye rolls, and apparent lack of belief from the care team, I felt like I was going crazy. I kept insisting that something was wrong with me, but I was repeatedly sent home.

Finally, after my third emergency department appearance on December eleventh, my x-ray report showed I had *four* vertebral fractures in my spine. The thoracic vertebrae at levels T3, T4, T5, and T6 appeared to be decimated by some force that compressed them to smithereens. They estimated I had lost four inches in height. I was told I would need surgery to reinflate the vertebrae and fill them with bone cement. *What the hell?* None of this made sense. But it was an answer. It explained my severe pain and deep knowing that something was wrong. I found out later that these fractures were visible on the *initial* x-ray, but were misread. So I jumped through hoops for days in extreme pain because of an error. I'm not knocking radiologists. I have a massive respect for radiology. That is one hell of a challenging field. But I had to endure multiple x-rays before it was read correctly as four fractures, despite them all being present on my initial scans, so it stings a little. And none of the other physicians on my team caught it either.

I met with the attending physician of the interventional radiology team so they could explain the surgical plan and get my consent for a kyphoplasty. This procedure involved a surgeon inflating a small balloon into my compressed T3–T6 vertebrae and injecting them with cement to regain height and decrease pain. I was immediately all in and ready to escape the intense pain. My parents were with me at this point and, thank goodness, asked appropriate questions since I was in and out of fugue states. This was, I'm sure, partly from the severe pain, but mostly from the unusual neurologic events I was experiencing (which my neurologist later identified as focal seizures). In the hospital, I continued having the full-body whooshes where I got the strange sensation of déjà vu, my vision darkened, the feeling of fainting would take over, and short-term memory loss immediately followed. The idea that these whooshes were actually seizures was thrown around a few times by my doctors, but they were laser focused on the fall and compression fractures, so I had to put a pin in that.

Along with fun neuro events, my left humerus (upper arm bone) decided it no longer wanted to stay in my shoulder joint and partially dislocated often—so often, in fact, that my labrum (shoulder cartilage) tore completely and I developed a reverse Hill-Sachs impaction fracture (meaning I broke the top of my humerus bone) through recurrent dislocations. My arm would literally fall out of the shoulder joint and I'd have to pop it back in place. But none of my hospital providers were concerned about this fact and told me that it was "an outpatient problem," meaning once I was discharged from the hospital I could see another doctor to explore what was wrong with my shoulder. I understood that my thoracic fractures were the primary problem, but why did no one care about my sudden neuro events and spontaneous shoulder dislocations? Sure, it wasn't an urgent, life-threatening problem, which is often the primary focus in the hospital, but this was one bizarre problem on top of another. Arms aren't supposed to just fall out of the shoulder they're connected to.

The surgery went well, and my pain dropped tremendously. I was sent home to recover in a new back brace (that was far less fashionable than my previous one) and some follow-up appointments with endocrinology, neurology, and sports medicine. Within a few days of being home, my pain crept back up and I was miserable. My last two weeks of 2018 were spent unsuccessfully trying to manage it.

January 1, 2019, was a strange day. I woke up on a mission to clean my condo, eat healthy, and start the new year right. I had a DEXA scan (which stands for dual x-ray absorptiometry) scheduled the following morning to measure my bone density to see if that was the underlying cause of my fractures, so I planned to go to sleep early that night. I remember so much of that day until a hard-stop moment later in the afternoon. Then it was as if my brain logged off and abruptly cut to me waking up on January second in severe chest and back pain. *Oh shit, I missed my appointment. Why am I in so much pain? Do I have new spinal fractures? How did I miss my appointment?* I was disoriented and started to cry. I called my parents in a panic not knowing what happened and they told me to go to the hospital, so I called my friend Caitrin to drive me. I felt deep in my core something was really wrong. At that moment, I had no memory of the day before. I looked to my phone for guidance and saw that I messaged my endocrinologist at 11:07 p.m. saying the following:

"One thing I forgot to mention during my appointment is that the week of my fractures I had three incidences of what now I think may have been focal seizures that have started happening again. They start with a feeling of déjà vu and then I get disoriented, lightheaded/dizzy, my heart races, my face gets flushed, and I almost feel like I could faint. They last one to two minutes, and they started happening again two days ago. I've had four in the last two days. Not sure if this is helpful, but it started the week my fractures happened, and prior to a month ago, this has never happened to me before. Also, please let me know when I should schedule a follow-up appointment. Thanks so much, Laura."

Then suddenly this memory catapulted to the forefront of my mind from the lost time of the night before. I remembered feeling the neuro event start, starting a timer on my phone, and grabbing a chair to sit in front of a mirror and watch what was happening. I guess my nurse brain attempted to observe any visual changes in my body and whether I was losing consciousness. I saw myself getting flushed and my breathing accelerating, but don't remember anything else. Regardless, it was intense. I don't remember messaging my doctor at all. I started to panic more.

Thankfully, once we got to the hospital Caitrin helped me advocate for myself by clearly communicating what was going on and filling in the blanks that I missed. The first tests they ran were blood tests for drugs and alcohol (shocker). Then, they sent me for a slew of labs, ordered an electrocardiogram and echocardiogram to check my heart function, assuming it was a myocardial infarction, also known as a heart attack. All came back negative. I was then sent for a chest CT scan, and lo and behold, I had a blood clot in my lung. This clot, technically called a pulmonary embolism, was in the lower right artery of my lung surrounded by cement. Apparently cement from my back surgery got into my bloodstream during the procedure and hardened in my pulmonary artery, the perfect anchor to a blood clot. I was flabbergasted. *How is all of this happening? Why do all these bad things keep happening to me?!* After relaying this news, I was admitted to the hospital and put on blood thinners and oxygen. My parents extended their stay in Denver to help me. My friends and coworkers visited me in the hospital. Everyone felt badly for me. And I felt badly for myself. I felt like I couldn't catch a break, and I was over it.

After my pulmonary embolism, the gamut of testing began. How could a thirty-year-old in seemingly good health spontaneously fracture four thoracic vertebrae and have unexplained neurological changes? I was tested for it all—bone cancer, celiac disease, osteogenesis imperfecta, heart disease, hypothyroidism, and so on. Finally some answers, right? Wrong. Every test came up negative. I was within normal ranges across the board. This continued after I went home and went on for months. I saw some top-tier specialists, and still, nothing came up conclusively explaining what happened. The dejection was real.

My mom suggested pursuing an out-of-state specialist diagnosis program that one of the top specialty hospitals in the country offered. I submitted my application and was approved. I had a date in May 2019 to see five different specialists over four days. I was relieved just to have hope. I planned to fly out with my parents to this specialty center and blocked off a week from work. But then, the perpetual pattern of things falling through for me came back swinging. In April, emails started trickling in that a specialist had to cancel. Then another. Then another. Then they "could no longer accommodate" my appointments. I was pissed—all that hope, just gone. After some extensive self-pity, I decided to spend that week in the mountains of Colorado. *I'm going to make the best of this*, I thought. I spent two days in the lovely town of Pagosa Springs with friends hitting up hot springs and relaxing. Then, I ventured by myself to Telluride. I had my three-hour-plus drive all planned out. I was going to leave early in the day, enjoy the drive along Million Dollar Highway (a gorgeous, yet at times treacherous drive), stop in Ouray for a few hours to hike and hot spring (yes, I use hot spring as a verb), and then head out to Telluride.

Just before the drive up to Million Dollar Highway, I saw a scenic lookout that had a bathroom (score!) and decided to pull off at Molas Pass. It was late May, and the ground was mostly snow-covered. I walked around a bit, took some breathtaking photos, and started heading back to my car. It was pretty slick from the snow, and I was in sneakers, so I hesitantly short-stepped my way back hoping to stay upright, when suddenly—boom. I smacked the ground and landed on my left wrist. I looked down, and the radial bone was jutting out to the side. *Oh fuck, oh fuck, oh fuck.* I knew it was broken. The sharp pain settled in. Then the panic. Then more pain. Then more panic. I was shaking from the adrenaline. I had no cell reception, so I had to pull it together and drive. I had to drive two hours by myself along a mountainous two-lane highway with one hand and no guardrails. I sat in silence for the entire drive along Million Dollar Highway. I kept trying to take deep breaths, but I was terrified. I cannot stress just how unpleasant driving along the side of a cliff with one hand was. But I somehow made it.

Apart from getting pulled over for speeding—but getting out of the ticket because I had a very crooked wrist and burst into tears from the stress—the rest of the drive was smooth sailing. I just had to make it to Telluride. My directions were taking me straight to the local hospital. Once I got there, I was greeted with a, "How can I help you?" by the emergency physician, which isn't typical, but this was a very small medical center.

I just pointed at my wrist and said, "I think we're broken here," and he escorted me back for an x-ray. The x-ray showed my radius was loaded with fractures. Of course it was. They hooked me up with some propofol and snapped it back in place. Thankfully, they reset it perfectly and I didn't need surgery, which surprised my Denver orthopedist, considering the number of fractures. I spent the next seven weeks in various splints and slings. Goodbye fun summer plans, hello immobilized wrist.

However, I was able to get free drinks in Telluride, so there was one positive.

After the wrist breaking, my endocrinologist referred me to a bone specialist in the Denver area. He was one of the few in the country to do bone biopsy testing for bone formation disorders like osteogenesis imperfecta, which is when you have very brittle bones that break without an obvious reason (think Samuel L. Jackson from *Unbreakable*, but a less severe form). So at least I had that to look forward to. I decided to continue with my life the best that I could until I obtained answers. I worked out with modifications with my personal trainer, I worked the front desk in my neonatal intensive care unit until I was out of the splint, and I carried on normally until that appointment a few months away. And I'm guessing you can imagine by now where this is going—Nowhere, population: 1. This particular bone specialist, one of the only to do this type of biopsy, retired before I could see him. The office he worked at told me they could not help me and they weren't aware of any other physicians who did this. I just laughed and thought, *Of course!* There was some rage release, but mostly the dichotomy of disbelief and actual belief that this was the way my life was going.

Once the initial emotional volatility passed, I did something shocking to myself that I had never done before. I let it go. I decided to keep on living. I was tired of searching for answers and getting nowhere except frustrated. I wanted to get back to some semblance of a normal life without searching for more problems. So I did. And it worked. I thought, *Hey, maybe this was just a bizarre health problem that resolved on its own. Maybe I'll be okay.* And then December 2021 happened, and I realized I had a lot much deeper going on that I needed to sift through.

Chapter 5

December 2021: When Shit Got Real

I began my trauma recovery journey in January 2022. New year, new me; am I right? Not exactly. I was freshly recovering from brain surgery after an accident in December 2021 that almost killed me—my fourth major accident in four years.

Let's rewind a bit.

It was December 4, 2021, and I was at the Christmas Market in Civic Center Park in downtown Denver with a group of friends and their kids. I was running around with one of the kids, spinning around and singing the lyrics to "Let It Go." Suddenly, I felt my balance start to go. I rapidly fought to regain it before succumbing to gravity. Instead, I smacked backward onto the hard surface of the Voorhies Memorial, a large structure composed of sandstone and granite at the park. I felt, and unfortunately heard, the loud smack of my skull against the stone. People ran over to me as I fumbled to get back up—and then the curtains fell. I'm 90 percent confident I didn't lose consciousness, but I definitely didn't log the memory of standing up and walking back to the rest of the group.

I sat down, and Amber, the mother of the girl I was playing with, immediately told me, "There's blood on your neck."

I said, "Oh yeah, I fell and hit my head, but I'm okay."

As I said this, I reached back to the area of my head that made contact, and my palm was covered in blood. My nurse brain (and injured brain) kicked in. "Heads bleed a lot," I added. "Not to worry."

Despite having blood-soaked hair and blood all over the collar of my coat, we were all reassured by my unshaken cognition. My friends knew nurses like me typically know when things are real emergencies—though we do tend to avoid the hospital at all costs. I'm a huge proponent of others going, but when it comes to my own health, I'm like, "Nah, I'm good."

The next morning, I felt and looked like absolute shit. I was nauseous as hell and threw up a few times, but I attributed that to a combination of the post-adrenaline effects of the fall, not eating much food that night, and drinking mulled wine. On top of that, I had dark bruising around my left eye and significant facial swelling. The impact of my head on the ground was just below my right ear, but my bruising and swelling was all around my left eye. This indicated a contrecoup injury, a head injury that is so hard the brain smacks into the skull on the opposite side of impact. In other words, my brain did a nice diagonal slingshot pattern from my lower right parietal bone to the back of my left eye. *Ouch* is right. I knew from my nursing school days that "raccoon eye" bruising is indicative of a skull fracture, but still asked my physical therapist friend, Kelsey, if I should go to the hospital.

I was hesitant to go, since I was

A. a nurse who worked in a hospital and preferred to not spend more time there,
B. cognitively "with it" still, so this probably wasn't *that* serious, and
C. in full-blown denial that it was something bad.

Kelsey freaked out after I told her about the facial bruising and demanded I go to the hospital immediately. So, you guessed it, I went to urgent care instead. That's my signature move. For all three of the most significant injuries I've had, I went to urgent care first instead of the hospital. Urgent care is where you go when it's not seemingly life-threatening, but you can't wait until tomorrow to find out. I'm sure it's entirely denial driven, but still, it is a pattern that took me this long and this level of severity to shake.

Before long, my boyfriend, Andrew, and I arrived at urgent care. I had vomited multiple times already that morning, and the nausea continued to worsen. The practitioner was puzzled at my seemingly normal cognitive state coupled with my jacked-up face, and recommended I go to the hospital. So much for my signature move. So, Andrew took me to the emergency department at the nearest hospital. It took a good while (about four more vomits' worth of time) to get seen.

With the resident physician, I went through what happened in great detail (understanding, as a nurse, the importance of a good history when it comes to guiding care direction) and explained that the main reasons I came in were the vomiting and eye bruising.

As the resident physician recommended, the most important test to determine the next steps was the neurological ("neuro" for short) exam. The neuro exam looks at the function of cranial nerves, reflexes, sensation, and motor responses to determine if there are deficits to neurologic function. This can help diagnose things like meningitis, Parkinson's, multiple sclerosis, and traumatic brain injuries.

I passed the neuro exam with flying colors. Every. Single. Time. Which totaled five times at that point. I was the champion of neuro exams. Every clinical provider who did a neuro exam on me was surprised, given my distressing facial appearance. But this was a good sign. My concussion couldn't be *that* bad; otherwise, it would be evident on the exam. The resident did agree the vomiting and bruising were worrisome, so along with some blood work, he went ahead and ordered a head computerized tomography (CT) scan. A CT scan is a diagnostic tool similar to an x-ray, but far more detailed—especially when it comes to internal bleeding. I figured it would come back normal, and I'd be diagnosed with a concussion and maybe a minor skull fracture.

Many hospitals nowadays give the patient access to their chart for lab or testing results. As a patient, and as a nurse, I do not believe this is the best idea. Sure, patients have the right to see their results as soon as they are available. However, whenever the results are less than ideal, they should be delivered by a medical team member who can explain everything before the patient has to piece together the terrifying (and, often, difficult to understand) results on their own. My fingers were glued to that refresh button on the hospital's patient portal that displayed results as they came in, desperate to see my CT scan results. I was hoping it would clear me of any major head injury and would allow me to go home.

Then the radiology report came in. When I read on the radiology report that I had a multicompartmental acute intracranial hemorrhage resulting in a large epidural hematoma, moderate subarachnoid hemorrhage, multifocal intraparenchymal hemorrhage, small subdural hemorrhage, parietal bone fracture, and leftward midline shift of my brain, I *panicked*. This meant I had a traumatic brain injury (TBI) and multiple areas of internal bleeding inside my skull that put pressure on my brain, a large area of pooled blood that also put pressure on my brain, and I broke a bone in my skull. There was so much bleeding on my brain that it caused my brain to shift eight millimeters inside a hard skull that has no give. This was serious. My heart dropped and then started beating so fast that the tachycardia (high heart rate) alarm sounded incessantly on my vitals monitor. I was hyperventilating and heading toward the deep panic spiral. One of the best things about Andrew is his ability to talk me off the ledge. He is skilled at calming me down and not letting me get ahead of myself. In this instance, it didn't really work, but that's no fault of Andrew's. This was an exceptionally severe situation.

A provider from the neurosurgery team came to see me to discuss the results. Despite my brain imaging, she was reassured by my clinical presentation and neuro exam (undefeated, baby). I knew nothing about neurology except for the basics of nursing school and what I saw from the babies in the NICU where I worked as a charge nurse. I thought, *Okay, even though this sounds serious, maybe this is healable on its own.* But those pipe dreams were quickly squashed when the attending physician walked in.

For those of you unfamiliar with a teaching hospital, there are levels of medical doctor hierarchy. It goes as follows: Intern is the first tier (first year out of medical school), then resident, then fellow, then attending. The attending physician is the supervising physician and the top expert. Oftentimes, the attending will pop their head in, but let the fellow or higher level resident manage the patient's care and they'll sign off. If the attending is your predominant care provider, that's a good thing because they are the top dogs. However, this can be a bad sign because your care is complex enough that it requires the highest level expert to manage. So when the attending physician came in to talk to me, I knew I was fucked.

It's surprising how vividly I remember this because I was in full-blown shock as she told me that the bleeds were pushing my brain toward my brainstem, which would ultimately kill me, and that I required an urgent craniotomy, which meant surgically removing part of my skull to expose my brain, draining the bleeds, replacing the bone, and placing plates and screws to keep the skull bone in place. Mic-drop moment. I felt everything in me light up with terror. She asked me if I understood, to which I replied, "Yes," and then she left. I remember turning to Andrew as the tears were forming and saying, "Oh my god. I might die." He did his damnedest to try and calm me down, holding my hand and reassuring me as best he could. After a brief and extremely appropriate freak-out, I wiped away my tears and channeled NICU Charge Nurse Laura, who is calm under pressure. I took a breath and just went into full-blown let's-get-it-done mode. I messaged my family and friends letting them know, *Hey, I'm okay, but I'm shortly going back for brain surgery. Andrew is your point of contact.* That must have been a fun text message for my recipients. I had waited to tell my parents because I kept thinking it was just going to be a concussion—no need to freak them out. My own unfortunate Uno reversal.

I was ready to get it over with. Let's fucking go. This was partly coming from a place of denial and shock mode, but also my years of rapid life-or-death emergent experiences in the NICU had built my brain for compartmentalizing trauma. I just wrapped it up into a nice little box and stuffed it in a corner so I could rationally prepare for what was to come. The amount of nurses, techs, nurse anesthetists, and doctors who asked me if I understood the severity of what was happening was almost funny. I put my game face on and fully absorbed what was happening so I could prepare for any and all outcomes, but I think my lack of emotion and heightened sarcasm were concerning to the staff. They thought I didn't understand the severity of the situation. But I got into my nurse mode where I was light on my feet and could critically think with the best of them. I also couldn't stop joking with everyone because my trauma processing is deeply rooted in sarcasm and self-deprecation.

As I'm consenting to all the risks of brain surgery, I'm cracking jokes about how this is not the ideal Sunday night for any of us. Everyone was probably thinking I was nearing the point of unraveling, but in actuality I was cool as a cucumber. The attending (who was amazing) explained how she would be leading my surgery. I met all of the nurses and providers who would be involved in my surgery. I was confident in them. I believed in them. Also I made enough jokes to be likable, so they weren't going to let me become a vegetable.

This was still latent COVID-19 times, so Andrew couldn't come with me to the post-anesthesia care unit (PACU), but they let him stay in the waiting room until my surgery was over. I couldn't tell you when I woke up in the PACU because that's the beauty of anesthesia. My first logged memory of consciousness was when the nurse came over and said everything went great, and I needed to hang out to make it through the recovery window. "Did someone call my boyfriend, Andrew?" I asked. The nurse said yes, and that Andrew stayed in the waiting room until they had to kick him out per the COVID visitor policy. I was in and out of dozing until they took me to the surgical trauma intensive care unit (STICU) in the very early morning hours of December sixth, and that was my home for the next few days.

My nurse identity and people-pleasing self enjoyed that I was an easy patient. I was STICU-designated by diagnosis, but my outward presentation sure wasn't. I was fully conscious. I didn't have an endotracheal tube with a ventilator to breathe for me, which is common after this type of surgery. Everyone was like, "Why aren't you worse?"

Between my lack of neurology knowledge and my injured brain, I tried to come up with some witty response, but ended up saying, "Ha. I don't know." After I was in the STICU for a few hours, it settled in a little how intense the prior twenty-four hours had been, but still didn't fully resonate. Andrew came in first thing the next morning, and I told him I must be fine since my brain could still make jokes—that must be a good sign. Which it was. I didn't die (obviously), but epidural hematomas are among the most life-threatening when it comes to traumatic brain injuries, and there was a good chance I wasn't going to be the same neurologically or wake up at all. It terrified me, so I kept those jokes rolling. I joked with everyone I could. I wanted to test my recovering brain, but also working in the hospital is so heavy, and I wanted to lighten everyone's mood. Between the scary understaffing and the actual horrific things that healthcare workers see, it gets brutal. If you can squeeze a laugh out of somebody, it can make all the difference in their day—even better when it's inappropriate. Just kidding, but maybe not depending on who you talk to. Thankfully, I had Andrew.

Ironically, Andrew had my parents. Did I mention that this was when Andrew met my parents for the first time? Yeah, there's that. Let's rewind a bit. Andrew and I started dating over the summer of 2021. Our relationship developed organically (minus the meeting on the dating app Hinge part, but that's reality in 2021). We meshed together so well and had the best time together. We were like-minded when it came to food, cocktails, travel, all the things. We just laughed all the time. Early in our dating adventure, we went to Hawaii, and I remember thinking, *Oh damn, he's looking like the one for me.* Things were going so well. And then, literal smack to the head, this happened. We had been dating for a few months when this accident occurred. Luckily, the meeting with my parents went well, though they were all concerned.

I was concerned myself, to be honest. It's a pretty crazy feeling when you realize you're potentially not going to wake up. I had so much faith in my surgical team, and I was confident surgery wouldn't kill me, but after signing consent after consent spelling out the death risk on top of letting the reality of the situation sink in, I was pretty terrified. I mean, it was clearing out a massive bleed on my brain that was compressing my brain toward my brainstem. Anything could have happened.

I knew my bleed was bad, but I didn't know how truly bad it was until I was in the STICU. Everyone was befuddled by how well I was clinically presenting (I was conscious and cracking jokes) yet how severe my brain bleeds were. They didn't match up. In the NICU, we see brain bleeds often, and they can be very devastating and can lead to death or lifelong disabilities. But in the STICU everyone said, "Have you seen your CT scan? I cannot believe you're conscious."

I knew it was a gnarly CT image, but fuck. It showed the large area of bleeds and how they were shifting the position of my brain. I had multiple people tell me that was the worst epidural hematoma they had ever seen. Epidural hematomas are when blood leaks into the dura mater (membrane directly under the skull that covers the brain). As the bleed gets bigger, it forms a pocket in the dura mater that pushes on the brain. Since the brain is softer than skull bones, the bleed can push the brain down toward the brainstem. If untreated, this can lead to damage that stops your breathing, leading to a coma, and eventually you die. Yeah, it was *bad*.

The first night, I slept great minus the neurological exams multiple times an hour for many hours immediately following surgery. No one to blame except classic post-operative protocol. Frequent neuro exams are given during the first few hours after surgery to ensure there isn't a sudden change in neurological status indicating something bad (like more bleeding or worsening brain damage). Between the damaged brain and high-stress day, all I wanted to do was sleep. The nurses apologized each time, but I was never upset. I understood. I'll take all the wake-ups to ensure I can keep talking, walking, and, well, stay alive.

I hope there's some nurses, doctors, and frankly anyone from the healthcare profession reading this book for many reasons. The main point that I'd like to echo originated from Dr. Jill Bolte Taylor in her book, *My Stroke of Insight*, and I can very much relate, so here goes. I cannot stress the importance of tacking on your exams with other providers, especially at a teaching hospital. I had my nurse assess me, then the intern, resident, fellow, and attending performed separate assessments on top of visits from physical therapy, occupational therapy, speech therapy, social work, and nursing assistant vitals checks. That's a lot of interrupted sleep for a brain desperately needing sleep to recover. I understand having frequent assessments to observe neurological status, but when I was being woken up constantly because everyone and their mother needed to assess me, it was less than ideal, especially when sleep is the most important factor when it comes to brain healing. If you are a nursing student, medical student, or intern, please go in with the nurse or doctor you are working with and bang out exams all together so your patient can sleep. It really does make a huge difference.

I spent three days in the STICU before being sent home. I was doing extremely well from an immediate post-brain-surgery standpoint outside of the pain and nausea. My parents flew in the morning after my surgery and, along with Andrew, helped me recover and adjust to life with a traumatic brain injury (TBI) and over forty stitches in my head. I was still in a state of semi-shock, and the gravity of it all was only sinking in so much. Then I got home and needed help with everything. I couldn't lift more than five pounds, couldn't have my head lower than my heart level (so no bending over), couldn't clean my incision, and couldn't drive. It was hard to go from independent Laura to dependent, injured-brain Laura. My tolerance for activity and the TBI symptoms was low. I felt awful. I was in so much pain. And it was starting to set in how the rug had been pulled out from under my life and I needed to find my footing. Thankfully, I had lots of help because I sure needed it. This was the beginning of a long and very challenging ride that completely changed the course of my life.

Chapter 6

Seize and Slow Bleed City

Exactly thirteen days after my brain surgery in December, another fun health scare decided to come my way. Andrew brought over Florida stone crabs to bring some positivity into my dark abyss of recovery. He was doing all the legwork as I sat like a helpless kid waiting to be fed. Suddenly, this intense rush of anxiety dropped in out of nowhere. Now, I've had more than a full year since this moment and numerous opportunities to describe this feeling to my doctors, and there is nothing else to accurately describe it other than a whoosh of impending doom and panic that took over my body. This was not like the whooshes of 2018 and 2019, though. This one felt like a wave dropping from my head all the way through my body that engulfed me in fear and dread that something bad was going to happen. As someone who's had the unfortunate luxury of lifelong anxiety, I knew this wasn't a panic attack. It was different. I told Andrew, "Something's wrong. I don't feel good." He did his best to calm me down and focus on the positive, but I knew deep in my core something bad was happening. Again.

I took out my contacts and moved over to the couch. I kept repeating, "Something's wrong. I just feel like something bad's about to happen." He kept reassuring me I was okay, which is a challenging skill that he mastered dealing with me through this process. My heart rate was elevated, and the urge to hyperventilate was hard to control as I struggled to take deep breaths. I rocked back and forth with my head in my hands, then I blacked out. Smash cut to me seeing paramedics walking through my condo with a gurney. In a panic I asked, "What's happening?"

Andrew told me calmly while looking at the floor, "You had a seizure."

What? I immediately started to cry. I was so disoriented. The post-seizure phase, called the postictal state, is a bizarre moment in time for your brain. The postictal state is the period after a seizure where the brain is recovering, and symptoms include confusion, fear, memory loss, and other cognitive deficits. I had a hard time answering the EMT's questions. I didn't know the date or the year or anything. I was panicking. I felt like my memory was completely erased.

They next asked, "Who is the president?"

I couldn't for the life of me figure out who it was, but I was able to say, "I don't know, but I know it's not Trump anymore." Which made them laugh. Yes, another point on the I'm-a-fun-patient scoreboard, which helped a little.

They took me to the nearest hospital, which thankfully was close enough that I could see it from my condo. Andrew met me there, and I was stuck in this deep state of shock and fear. He told me that I started aggressively clenching my jaw, my eyes rolled back, and I went into a full-blown grand mal seizure. A grand mal seizure entails loss of consciousness and intense muscle convulsions for minutes that to an onlooker can feel like an hour. He caught me as I started to go down toward the ground and called 911. He looked textbook-definition traumatized. I kept trying to make jokes (as I do), but he wasn't having it. Rightfully so, he thought I was going to die.

We held hands as we waited for the results of my CT scan, which I could only imagine would be bad. It was at this point I told him I loved him for the first time. I was very afraid of saying, "I love you," out loud. I knew I loved him, though. We just hadn't said it to each other yet. So right after I had a traumatic event seemed like the opportune moment. He told me he loved me, too, and held my hand tighter. Thankfully, my CT scan and labs looked good, and there was nothing else wrong. After an observation period, they sent me on my way with some anti-seizure medication, and I hoped for the best, but expected the worst. I had good reason; am I right? Things kept going wrong for me, and I had succumbed to that being my area of expertise.

December was plenty rough—a traumatic brain injury, brain surgery, seizure, multiple emergency department visits, and more. But January 2022 was when it really kicked into high gear. Throughout the month of December, I had fairly frequent CT scans to check the healing progress of my leftover hematoma (pool of blood that remained on my brain). All were very routine. I'd have the scan, see a provider from the neurosurgery team, hear them essentially say, "Moving right along," and I'd go home. But my January fifth follow-up was a bit different. The attending physician who performed my surgery came in, which wasn't typical from the previous visits. She told me my scan that day was considerably worse. I had developed a new subdural hemorrhage, meaning a new area of active bleeding on my brain. After my surgery, there was an underlying subdural hematoma (meaning blood that already clotted) present in my brain measuring eight millimeters after surgery. Now it was twelve millimeters, indicating that the hematoma was now a hemorrhage. Now, this sounds small, sure, but subdural hemorrhages are the slow internal bleeds that show no symptoms until you start slurring your words, have a hard time staying awake, or you straight-up drop to the ground and die.

It was a punch straight to the gut. I was going backward yet again in the healing process. The attending told me I had to rest like I'd never rested before because the alternative was another craniotomy. I felt myself deflating and searching desperately for words as I stared back at the attending. She gave me objective instructions to not leave my home, no more walks, only extremely minimal activities around the house with breaks every ten minutes, no screen time, and basically be on a modified bed rest. The thought of being chained to my bed, unable to forget about my problems with hiking, travel, or fun of any kind, was horrifying.

The next move was to have another CT scan in four weeks or sooner if I got worse. "How will I know if it's getting worse?" I asked. She told me if my symptoms got worse to call her office and schedule another appointment for a scan. Or if they got really bad, where I started slurring my words or losing consciousness, to go to the emergency department. *Holy shit.* I walked out of the neurosurgery office stunned and emotionless, and once I got in the car, the tears started flowing. I didn't want to tell anyone because telling people made it real. I so badly wanted to just be better—to be able to exercise, be around people, and resume my normal life. But I couldn't. I had to pull the emergency brake and come to a screeching halt. How do you go from doing nothing to doing *nothing?* This was my actual nightmare—no walks outside, no organizing my condo, no lifting anything, just doing nothing above the most basic tasks of daily living with scheduled breaks.

For the next week, I was frozen in a perpetual breakdown. If I wasn't crying, I was staring at the wall wishing I had died already. I imagined that I never went to the hospital and died in my sleep. I didn't want to kill myself; I just truly wanted my existence to be over. I had zero hope. I was on the hamster wheel of dread, and there was no way to get off.

Recovery from a TBI is already awful, with frequent headaches, difficulty concentrating, poor short-term memory, and difficulty finding words to speak. Healing recommendations are no screens, minimal stimulation, and lots of rest. That wasn't how I operated, and it was torture for me. But now I had to double down on rest and boredom even more to hopefully avoid another brain surgery. I questioned everything about myself. *What is wrong with me? Why do only bad things always happen to me? I'm such a piece of shit. I must deserve this.* The thoughts were setting up camp in my brain and were in a constant loop.

I thought this was going to actually kill me. I had to keep my thoughts calm and not freak out about getting worse. I was in a persistent state of worry and borderline panic when a headache got a little worse or I felt a ping of nausea. Any neurological symptoms that worsened in any way sent my thoughts into pure chaos. These symptoms were also a part of the TBI and craniotomy healing process, so I lived in a constant state of fear.

Had the attending not given me clear objective instructions, I would have continued overdoing it and required another brain surgery. That was the Laura Renner way—just push, push, push. But this time, I had to just sit and listen to my thoughts. I had no other choice, and the beginning was brutal. I cried and made myself feel like such a piece of shit. Then finally I reached the point after many, and I mean many, breakdowns that the only way out of this was to completely dismantle my way of thinking. Otherwise, it would, without question, lead to my own demise, whether it was death or severe cognitive decline. Neurology is funny in that it's all reactive. You have to see what symptoms develop, see if they go away, and then take action. So on top of being up to my neck in my own thoughts, I had to decipher whether my symptoms were worsening or typical healing changes.

Which really made the Stevens-Johnson syndrome saga that developed soon after a real treat.

What is Stevens-Johnson syndrome, you ask? It is a rare, life-threatening allergic reaction to certain medications that starts with flu-like symptoms, then escalates to skin rashes, blisters, and inflammation all over your body. Yep, I had that. Just when you thought it couldn't get any worse, right? I had started a new anti-seizure medication, lamotrigine, after my seizure, and I loved it. That's a weird thing to say about a medication, but most anti-seizure medications make you feel sleepy, dizzy, irritable, and nauseous. Lamotrigine allowed me to feel like an energized human again, which was so welcomed after my brain injury that sucked all the energy out of me. Finally, something good! Nope, I was sadly mistaken.

About two weeks into my treatment with lamotrigine, I noticed in the shower that my legs and arms were completely covered in hives. It was as if they appeared from nowhere. My critical thinking switched on. I hadn't changed my laundry detergent or skin products. I hadn't eaten anything new. My days were so routinely unchanged from being couch-ridden. Stevens-Johnson syndrome kept blaring like a fire alarm through my brain. But I knew how rare it was, so I was miraculously able to keep my freak-out to a simmer. I took some deep breaths and told myself to watch it for a little while and go from there. Well, that plan lasted all of a few hours when the rash exploded all over my body. I called the local nurse hotline to see if my moderate anxiety needed to escalate to full-blown panic. The nurse assured me that no, it was not Stevens-Johnson syndrome. That usually develops within the first week, and my symptoms were too mild. Thank God. I was advised to take some diphenhydramine (generic Benadryl) and that it should go away in a few days.

Those next few days, however, were real nail-biters because everything got worse. I took diphenhydramine around the clock and was halving my lamotrigine dose because I was mildly nonstop panicking despite being "fine." I woke up in the middle of the night to pee and saw that my eyes were bright red. And I mean bright red like pink eye on steroids. I tried to go back to sleep for a nanosecond, then pulled the trigger and called the nurse hotline again. I went through all the details and even sent photos of my eyes, arms, and legs to show what was going on. But again, I was assured that no, it still didn't sound like Stevens-Johnson syndrome. I didn't buy it. Still, what else could I do? I hung up.

That's when everything really went to hell in a handbasket in my body. My lips doubled in size and split open. My mouth straight-up hurt. Sores developed on the inside of my mouth and gums. My tongue became so inflamed it could barely fit in my mouth. And to top it off, I began experiencing chest pain. At this point, I had no choice but to go to the hospital. It was a Saturday night in the emergency department in downtown Denver, which was complete chaos. I finally got into a room and explained to the healthcare team what was going on with me.

For hours, I went through my symptom progression, stating I was worried about Stevens-Johnson syndrome, but was still met with resistance. It was baffling. They could see my physical symptoms. I was on a medication that can cause this reaction. There was nothing else to explain it. I felt crazy. *What if it gets worse and I suddenly get really sick? What is this doing to my healing brain? Why won't anyone believe me?* This seemed like a straightforward reaction of Stevens-Johnsons syndrome, yet they kept brushing it off. The attending physician and resident suggested maybe it was mono (mononucleosis, a virus that commonly affects teens). I was confused. I explained I had mono in high school (most people only get mono once), but they still tested me for it. It was negative (this was a shocker to everyone except Andrew and me). They then suggested it was an allergic reaction to a new detergent or skincare product, to which I immediately replied, "No. I haven't changed any of my products in the last month. That's not it." That tidbit of information didn't matter. They sent me home and told me to keep taking antihistamines and that it "should get better." I was dumbfounded. No one believed me that this was Stevens-Johnson syndrome? Was this for real?

Thankfully, my neurologist believed me. He took one look at me and within five seconds said it was Stevens-Johnson syndrome and to stop taking lamotrigine immediately. I finally took a breath of relief. This relief, however, was short-lived because your girl over here went crazy. Lamotrigine is also a mood stabilizer used to treat bipolar disorder and requires a slow wean off the drug to allow your brain to adjust to the neurotransmitter changes. Because of the lovely Stevens-Johnson syndrome, I had to stop taking it immediately to stop this potentially life-threatening reaction. So that led me into a mini-psychosis. Nonstop panic attacks. Sobbing constantly. Frequent pacing through my condo looking behind every door because I was convinced someone else was in my home (which was inaccurate). Calling 911 worried about my life, but afraid if paramedics came they would lock me up in a mental health facility, so I'd hang up.

Yeah, it was bad. I was very unwell. That's why they tell you on pharmaceutical commercials to not stop taking psych medications immediately because it throws your brain into a tailspin. After a weekend that felt like the longest weekend of my life, I was able to reach my neurologist to get an anti-anxiety medication. Mind you, this was still in the world of COVID-19, so the earliest I could see my primary care physician, or any medical provider with prescribing authority, was over a month from that date. So the cocktail of clonazepam, time, and mindful deep breathing finally got me out of the psychosis woods. Needless to say, between the new bleed, Stevens-Johnson syndrome, and the never-ending cycle of breakdowns, January wasn't my month.

Part 2

The Shift to Healing and Awareness

Chapter 7

The Eye-Opening February

When I say I was at a low point, boy, it was low. I was two months out from the craniotomy, yet I felt entrenched in stagnation. Sadness was replaced with emptiness. I was living a miserable existence. *Why couldn't I have just died?* I obsessed over that thought for a long time. I didn't understand why I was living to suffer. I believed on a deep level that I would be broken forever. Each day consisted of worry spirals waiting for the next bad thing to happen. Until one day in February, something shifted, and I had this sudden change of heart. A switch flipped in my brain, and I decided, *Fuck this. I'm not letting worrying about my health and the bad things control me anymore. I need a mindset shift, and it needs to start right now.* And then I kicked it into high gear.

I was determined to get back to old Laura in a brain recovery way, but a new Laura state of mind. So I went into full-blown healing mode. I listened to all the audiobooks on brain healing, trauma, and mindset shifting that I could find from sunup to sundown. I read as much as my recovering brain would tolerate. I listened to podcasts for mindset work and spirituality with headphones in the waiting rooms for my appointments. I doubled down on my speech and occupational therapy frequency and did an hour of homework every day. I dove head first into a twenty-week personal development program. I intensively explored how I became this way and went deep into the roots of my childhood to expose origins. I found meditations on YouTube and spent hours a day visualizing my healing and a better life. I started taking another anti-anxiety medication and focused on redirecting my anxious thoughts. And then it just clicked. I truly *believed* I was healing. I believed I was getting better. I believed that I could do whatever I set my mind to. And it manifested as rapid improvements in my life.

I was able to find words when speaking instead of saying, "Um, um, um," until I gave up. I was able to do the highest level math and problem-solving exercises my speech therapist could find when before I struggled with basic addition. I was able to take away the constant need for noise-canceling earplugs and rose-colored glasses. My short-term memory came back. I experienced fewer headaches. I wasn't needing twelve shots of espresso a day to function. And most importantly, I felt happy. I was enthusiastic about my healing. I was enjoying my days. The more I practiced positive affirmations, visualizations, and journaling my feelings, the better I felt.

I accepted that it wasn't going to be a steady life of feeling great and that I needed professional help to guide me through the deep trauma healing I desperately desired. Based on my personal research and experiences,

I realized that Somatic Experiencing therapy and eye movement desensitization and reprocessing, also known as EMDR, were paramount to my healing journey. Both somatic therapy and EMDR are modalities to treat PTSD.

Somatic therapy, also known as Somatic Experiencing, was developed by Dr. Peter Levine as a method for resolving stuck physiological states in the body resulting from trauma. The Ergos Institute of Somatic Education (also founded by Dr. Levine) explains Somatic Experiencing on their website much more eloquently than I can, so here is their description:

> The SE™ approach facilitates the completion of self-protective motoric responses and the release of thwarted survival energy bound in the body and nervous system, thus addressing the root cause of trauma symptoms. This is approached by gently guiding clients to develop increasing tolerance for difficult bodily sensations and suppressed emotions, building their capacity for containment and resilience. Beginning in the 1970's, Peter's explorations into how animals deal with threat led to the development of the Somatic Experiencing® method (SE™), a method that is highly effective in dealing with the effects of overwhelm on our nervous system. SE™ is a clinical methodology based upon an appreciation of why animals in the wild are not traumatized by routine threats to their lives, while humans, on the other hand, are readily overwhelmed and often

subject to long-lasting traumatic symptoms of hyperarousal, shutdown, and dysregulation.[1]

Eye movement desensitization and reprocessing is an evidence-based therapy dating back to the 1980s founded by Dr. Francine Shapiro. It targets unprocessed memories, and shifts the way they are stored and the associated symptoms they display. It's really fascinating how it works. During an EMDR session, the client is guided to focus on an emotionally disturbing memory as their eyes move from side to side. These eye movements essentially unblock the brain's traumatic memory network so that emotional processing can occur and emotional distress can be eliminated.

I wanted to use all the tools to heal from every angle. I was ready to dive in head first to Somatic Experiencing and EMDR. I was finally over the hurdle of seeing my trauma for what it was and moving past it. I knew it was going to be a perilous ride for my mind, but also that it was absolutely necessary to heal my deep wounds that kept showing up as patterns of awful occurrences. And that was so scarily accurate.

---

[1] https://www.somaticexperiencing.com/somatic-experiencing, accessed 3-10-2023.

Chapter 8

My Inner Critic and Inner Hardass

Understanding my past helped me heal from the trauma of the present. There was so much I forgot about, ranging from truly bad events to even minor moments that hurt me. EMDR was a massive game changer for becoming aware of how my past experiences conditioned my adult life. The majority of my EMDR sessions focused around identifying two central themes—I'm a bad piece of shit, and I need to be hard on myself. My therapist identified these as my Inner Critic and Inner Hardass. Some EMDR sessions brought up repressed memories, and others connected the origins of core beliefs about myself to specific memories. So many deep-seated beliefs about yourself often stem out of single moments in time that compound each other. EMDR opened my thinking to how childhood moments that elicited feelings of fear, shame, or letting people down became the foundation of my core beliefs about myself.

I started working with a Hakomi therapist in May 2022 who had a strong background in EMDR and somatic therapy. The Hakomi Method centers around mindfulness, the mind-body connection, and supporting disconnected parts of yourself to unify as a whole. The sessions began with centering myself, dropping into my breath, and actually feeling the sensations in my body—not making changes to them, but just noticing how my body felt in that moment and letting those feelings guide the session. Most of the time, I felt chest tightness, scattered energy, and racing, anxious thoughts that pulled me out of my body and into my head.

Come to find out, I lacked awareness in all areas of connection to my body and how disconnected parts of myself were. So this therapy was super effective. The initial draw of EMDR and Somatic Experiencing therapy was what pulled me in, but the results are why I stayed. Early on in EMDR therapy, I realized my entire thought structure was based on outer influences telling me I needed to be productive and successful; otherwise, I was a worthless piece of shit. But I realized in therapy that I don't need to be productive to have worth. Other people move through life without this self-pressure; why can't I?

Pulling apart these ideas sends you into a bit of a tizzy, forcing you to ask the question, "Then who am I?" But here's the kicker. I was not these thoughts. I felt deep in my core that these thoughts were the foundation of who I was, but they were absolutely not. They were a product of the parts I neglected. The parts that were bad. The stories that enveloped me in misery and worry. That

I'm unloveable, stupid, lazy, ugly, and worthless based on mistakes I made or how perceptions from others made me feel. I buried them deep so they'd never surface. I piled on shame and extreme negative self-talk as a means to keep them down. And because of this methodology, I taught myself to use shame and hurtfulness as a deterrent from the bad things.

Our brains protect us from threats by making us feel terrible enough to avoid them, and, whew, my brain was really good at that. I learned that my Inner Critic was exceptionally harsh. And interestingly enough, that's a defense mechanism intended to keep you safe, but it sure as hell doesn't feel like it. It feels like when something gets stuck in my throat and I can't swallow, which leads to that brief panic of, *Am I going to choke?* Then follows the feeling of, *Why was I dumb enough to take a bite that big? If I hadn't, this wouldn't have happened and I'd be fine. Instead, my eyes are watering and I'm coughing nonstop, and that's all my fault. If I had done better, this wouldn't have happened.* So now I'm filled with regret about how I stupid I am instead of just dealing with the choking. Those thoughts follow even after the moment has passed, and that's where the deep worthlessness begins. I asked numerous times in therapy, "Doesn't everyone have a harsh inner critic?" only to be told, "No," repeatedly. I finally realized that being so excessively harsh on myself wasn't healthy and that I not only wanted, but needed, to change.

As I mentioned before, the Inner Critic and Inner Hardass ran the show in my brain. My therapist helped me identify these two roles through examples in EMDR, and, boy, are they dominant. The Inner Critic tells me all that's wrong with me, which is everything. How fat I am every time I see my reflection. How huge my abdomen is. How my left eye is droopy and makes me look ugly. How my under-eye wrinkles are pronounced and that's only going to get worse. How my posture is trash. Every time I looked in the mirror, these thoughts flowed out as a stream of consciousness. None of them ever focused on positive, self-affirming, or good things about me. And then came the general shit-talking to myself. *Why did you say something so stupid? You're such an idiot. Why do people even like you? I'm such a dumbass. I'm truly a bad person. No wonder bad things happen to me because I'm such a piece of shit.* The list is endless and horrifying to remember.

The Inner Hardass was the especially persistent one here. That's all the shoulds. Shoulds dominated my thoughts by a landslide. *I should empty the dishwasher right now. I should order my face serum so I don't run out. I should go to a spin class tonight even though I feel bad, because otherwise I'm lazy. I should make plans with so-and-so. I haven't seen them in a while, and they might think I'm a bad friend. I should schedule my next haircut right now.* And so on. And the clincher is my Inner Critic says they all must happen *right now* or I'm a failure. I will pop up out of meditation to schedule my cat's annual checkup. I will stop doing a task to start another task, then realize I should do something else, and I'll interrupt that task. It's a constant state of shoulds that are so seemingly important that I must come to a screeching halt and complete whatever it is immediately.

My Inner Hardass loves cracking that whip. I functioned best under pressure (or so I thought), and the Inner Hardass constantly alerted me to everything I absolutely had to do. If I had a free second, I looked at my task list on my phone and checked if I could knock anything out to free up some time, but then whenever I thought I had free time, my Inner Hardass would flood my thoughts with other things. I never realized how cyclical this was until my therapist pointed this out. I thought this part of me was a good thing—motivating and productive as hell. But in actuality, it prevented me from being present, listening to my intuition, and having control.

Learning about intuition was quite mind-blowing for me. I had zero concept of intuition. I was so far removed from it that I couldn't imagine how it even felt. Many people can relate to feeling something is off, even if they can't explain why. It just feels off. That never resonated with me until recently. I learned about intuition in my mindset and personal development work. I could understand it as a possible concept, but it felt so foreign to me. When I sat and thought about what I wanted to do next, all these thoughts of, "I need to go to the grocery store," "I should stretch since I'm so inflexible," "I haven't done my brain exercises today," "I should do laundry," and whatnot immediately popped up. That's not intuition; that's still rooted in my conscious thoughts, but that's all I could hear. My body couldn't take the lead because the Inner Hardass was the CEO, leaving no opportunity to lean into what I felt like doing or exude any free will. I had to be disciplined and hardworking always; otherwise, the Inner Critic said I was a piece of shit, right? Wrong. But that's what old Laura believed wholeheartedly. You had to be hard on yourself because then you were productive, and if you were not productive, you were a piece of shit.

It is no exaggeration that every single therapist and coach I worked with through the years has said, "You're so hard on yourself!" And I wore that as a badge of honor. Hell yeah, I'm hard on myself—that's how you win. That's how I'm successful and prove my value! Cue the wrong answer buzzer. Until this realization, I had no clue how warped my seemingly positive way of thinking was. I was so proud of being hard on myself. But after therapy, it turned into a symbol of shame. Here I was, holding up like a trophy the very thing that was holding me back. There's still a good amount of shame there for me. It's a work in progress fully releasing the Inner Hardass and the pain it brought to my inner child and current adult self. I feel so ashamed that I treated myself this way for so long—most of my life, unfortunately. The wiring of my brain was stuck in a loop of "You're bad," and, damn, it requires so much intentional work to change that Inner Critic.

Breaking the cycle felt like losing myself since it was such a large part of me. I thought the Inner Hardass and Inner Critic were me, but the deepest and most painful parts of us that have been neglected and shamed are the parts that are most ingrained in our thoughts.

The overarching theme of the Inner Hardass stemmed out of the principle that I was never good enough and I could have always done something better. The shoulds came in strong here when thinking about all of my past actions and how I should have done them differently. I could never look back at something with a kind lens. It was always, "I should have ordered the other entree that would have been better." Every experience was clouded with thoughts of how if I did them differently, they would have been better, which essentially always implied that everything I did was wrong or not good enough.

Recognizing that all my thoughts toward myself were pretty severe was a major breakthrough that took all the way until July 2022 to realize. And by recognizing, I mean having multiple therapists explain it over, and over, and over again until I could actually hear it. Surprise! My conscious and subconscious hard-stopped these notions from being my reality for many months of trauma therapy. These were the deepest wounds for me to clear.

Telling myself I'm a work in progress stings. That perfectionist, ambitious, type three Enneagram can't be a work in progress. The Enneagram is a personality-typing system and type threes are achievers, success-oriented, and image-conscious. Very much me. So being a work in progress was not allowed. I always have to be on. I always have to be the best. But this is radical self-acceptance in the works over here, so watch me go.

After three months of EMDR and Somatic Experiencing therapy, I reached a level I never thought I was capable of. I had been so nose-to-the-grindstone with my career and life. I was escaping and afraid to face my true self, unaware of who my true self even was. I had built mountain-size hurdles to get away from knowing who I was. Thinking that my negativity, my self-loathing, and my bullying tactics toward myself were who I was at my core, I thought that was all of who I was. I'm sure this is the case for most of us, autopiloting through life with no clue of who we are and what we truly want out of life. We develop these learned behaviors and establish this sense of thinking that our thoughts are who we are. But it's so false. We don't give ourselves the opportunity to just sit and think, *What do I want? Who am I? What am I seeking out of my life?* The answers to those questions are who we are, but we never allow ourselves to ask them. I never asked, and I sure wasn't that person. I never gave myself an opportunity to think. For me, thinking meant all the shoulds and the self-hatred, the Hardass and the Critic, just spiraling into darkness within my mind. But that was just my scared inner child attempting to protect me, shielding me from embarrassment, being an outcast, being disliked, keeping me "safe." It was a learned thought pattern that I taught myself over thirty-plus years to get by in the best way I knew how. It all stemmed from learned behaviors. We don't realize just how much our thoughts are based on learned behaviors. It's not just how we tie our shoes or our religious beliefs. It's our thoughts, how we perceive others, and how we talk to ourselves. And, wow, the way I talked to myself was brutal. Of all of the dysfunctional one-sided relationships I've had in my life, no one has ever talked to me as viciously as I did to myself.

One of the reasons that the Inner Hardass exists in me is to be my protective mechanism. It points out the bad qualities in myself to try and protect myself from having someone else point them out first, which backfires and has the opposite effect by putting pressure on me and making those qualities feel worse. In a healthier thought capacity, I would be kinder to myself and encourage positivity. I would notice the good in me as well as the bad. I have a really hard time not getting stuck in the shoulds and whys, and on some level that's how I protect myself. I have created this story of always pointing out the flaws and the bad, which stems from parents, grandparents, teachers, coaches, and peers in my childhood. My ego points them out as an attempt to keep me safe, but instead it sends me into spirals.

I never learned how to regulate my emotions and allow them to mature while growing up, so I stayed stuck in the pattern I learned in childhood, which was the thought spiral. The spirals became my comfort zone. That was the only way I knew how to respond—feeling out of control, panicking, then letting those thoughts feed off each other and get worse and worse. I was so used to going deep into the rabbit holes of "I'm bad" and "bad things will happen to me," and sadly, it became a comfortable and frequently utilized neural pathway for me. We'd rather be comfortable and in pain than uncertain and okay. That comfortable pain is safe. When I was healing from my brain surgery, back surgery, and the snowboarding accident, I was in a frequent state of thought spirals. That's because it felt comfortable. I was used to the negativity.

Our brain is biologically wired to focus on the negative as a primitive means of survival. It's called the negativity bias. Remembering the fear of a lion chasing you after you stumble into its den is a safety mechanism to keep you alive and pass on your genetic code. Since early humans were wired to survive and pass on their genes, this was a valuable trait. Today, most negative threats are emotional not physical; however, they can have the same deleterious effects. The neuroscience evidence of negativity bias is extensive. Psychologist and neuroplasticity expert Dr. Rick Hanson uses the analogy that "the brain is like Velcro for negative experiences, but Teflon for the positive ones."[2] In addition, the amygdala (that's the fire alarm when there's perceived danger) uses more neurons for negative stimuli than positive. And since it is a large emotional regulator, that means your brain is using more neural activity, which means more brain power for negativity, and therefore perpetuating the cycle.

Don't worry, though; there is hope. And that hope is called neuroplasticity. Neuroplasticity is the brain's ability to adapt based on utilization of neural pathways (connected neurons that work together). Neuroplasticity is in action when you learn a new language or pick up a

---

[2] https://www.rickhanson.net/overcoming-negativity-bias/, accessed 3-10-2023.

new instrument, but this can also mean negative effects. You know the phrase, "Use it or lose it"? That also applies to your brain. If you stop speaking that new language or put down that instrument, your brain will forget those skills. But it also means you are capable of change. Neuroplasticity can apply with TBIs (which is very evident in my case with learning how to do math and speak full sentences again), but also with rewiring your response patterns away from the negative and toward the positive, like my therapy did for me. There is a plethora of research centered around neuroplasticity available online, so feel free to nerd out on that at your leisure.

But back to my negative brain. As my immature childhood brain responded negatively to almost everything, those neural pathways strengthened to a Hulk-like level that has required constant intention to rewire. This has looked like questioning my thoughts, choosing to redirect them, and spending multiple times a day focusing on positive affirmations. EMDR exposed me to my reliance on the Inner Critic and Inner Hardass pathways, but also showed me that I could actually change them. You don't have to let your past wiring dictate your future. And I sure as hell am not.

Chapter 9

Woes of the Healing Journey

Being on this healing journey is a lot like running. Well, running for people who aren't runners, myself included. You start feeling the pain early on, and you're like, "Forget this. I want to stop," but you hope if you go a little further it won't suck as badly. As you're a little further into the run, you settle into the sweet spot of, "Okay, I think I can do this," and you hit that comfortable stride. Soon after, you're back to the, "Nope, I can't do this. This is hard," and you are hell-bent on stopping. This is where a lot of us usually throw in the towel.

So what if you say, "I just need to make it to that next stop sign." Then the stop sign comes and you say, "Okay, legs, let's make it to the next stop sign." This is that really tough part where your body is saying, "Respectfully, fuck off and end this," but you know how good it will feel to hit that next stop sign. And maybe you keep playing this game until you make it to your original destination. Even if you don't make it that far, you can feel proud of pushing yourself further than you thought you could. And you know you're better for it in the end.

That's the healing process in a nutshell. You have to constantly throw yourself over the next hurdle to what feels like the sweet spot, but it's not. You know something else challenging is about to jump right in front of your path. However, with time and practice, you get used to it.

You find comfort in the discomfort. So instead of getting tripped up by the hurdles, you embrace the challenge knowing how damn good it feels to get beyond it. I have had many moments of wondering if I am crazy. Is it crazy to explore deeper into the pain and trauma? I didn't want to keep reliving when I almost drowned. I didn't want to feel the intense anxiety and fear I felt throughout much of my childhood. But it's absolutely not crazy. Healing has been worth every second of misery I've experienced along the way.

The more I looked inward to work on myself, the more messed up I felt. Self-improvement is no joke. That hyper self-awareness shines a spotlight on everything you think, say, and do. The more aware you are of your flaws, the more intimidating it is to fix them. It's quite the paradox. I had many moments of hating myself more after opening the doors for the Inner Critic and Inner Hardass intentionally, facing them head on so I could challenge them right back, saying, "Fuck you," to them when I have a laundry list of to-dos, but choose rest for myself instead. Moments like this allowed me to realize I don't hate myself. I'm lucky to be in this process. Yeah, you heard me. I am lucky to learn about myself and grow more every day.

Now, let's be clear. I've had countless moments along this healing journey of thinking I don't want to do this anymore. Let me go back to living without awareness. Ignorance is bliss, baby. But then I always bring myself back to this moment in time with my ex-husband. We were sitting on a very uncomfortable couch at couples therapy, and tears were streaming down my face. Our therapist looked at my husband and said, "Look at Laura. She's crying. She doesn't want to cry, but she's allowing herself to feel her emotions. You've built up such a wall that you're unable to even access your emotions. With a lot of deep work, you can get to this place of accessing your emotions."

And he took a short moment, then said, "I don't want to do that." He didn't want to face his traumas like I did.

That was our last counseling session. I walked out of there thinking it was time to get the hell away from this person. When I reflect on that moment and his flat-out refusal to face his traumas, it reminds me why I'm doing this. It's not that it's easy because it sure isn't. It can be brutal. But it's what I need to grow and live the way that I want. It's what I need to heal. It's the only path for me to move forward. It's the only way for the health problems to stop. It's the only way I can truly love myself. So I'm doing it, and there's no looking back.

Chapter 10

Nervous System Regulation

Everyone's journey will focus on something different, but I realized my key to successfully healing was in regulating my nervous system. It wasn't like that at first. Whenever authors or podcasters discussed nervous system regulation, it wouldn't land with me at all. What the hell is nervous system regulation? I researched it, and it still didn't click. I'm sure this was a combination of protecting myself and being out of touch with my body. My walls of disconnection were so high when it came to my body. After what felt like neverending repetition of researching nervous system regulation, it finally clicked.

Nervous system dysregulation is when you start losing control of your mindset and let the feelings of anxiety, sadness, or anger completely take the wheel. So the ability to calm yourself down from a heightened state, push away the spiral, and get back on the no-sweetie-I'm-in-control train is, in fact, nervous system regulation. It pulls you out of the acute stress response of fight or flight. This isn't something most people do naturally. There are truckloads of research-based tools to regulate your nervous system, such as deep breathing, meditation, Emotional Freedom Technique (EFT), journaling, exercise, getting outside, and so on. When I realized that I can be in control when I get anxious or upset and use tools to calm myself down that actually work, I was blown away. I never thought that something could dial down my spirals or fully yank me out of them. I had accepted once a negative spiral began, I'd be in the air with it for a while.

Not only was I a super anxious kid, but I was a crier. I was the champion of crying. I cried over everything because I was constantly afraid and didn't know how to manage it. Regardless of what anyone said to get me to stop, I just couldn't. This was all a matter of nervous system dysregulation. I never learned how to effectively calm myself down. Once I felt that drop in my stomach, increase in heart rate, or welling up of tears in my eyes, it was over. I had no idea how to bring myself out of those feelings. So I just cried, even as an adult. For someone who prides themselves on being strong, this was such a kick to the back of the knee. How can I be strong and cry? "You can't," is what I would say. Now I know that crying doesn't mean I'm weak.

I still struggle with it. It's hard to expose your vulnerability, but it's even harder not to when you don't know how to control your nervous system response. Thank goodness for tools and education. Hallelujah. I have dabbled with countless tools and have dialed in what works best for me. The key to regulating your nervous system is finding what works for *you*. It is very specific. I can tell you to dance every time you're upset (yes, that is a regulation tool), but if that doesn't work for you, then you won't move the needle.

I personally love Emotional Freedom Technique (EFT) because it's like psychological acupressure. EFT utilizes tapping your fingers on specific acupuncture points while verbally working through your feelings out loud. EFT expert Brad Yates explains it beautifully as "a very effective method of physically resetting the body's fear response by tapping on energy meridians throughout the body while talking through and resolving emotional resistance or trauma."[3] It's some powerful stuff for me. I don't just reserve tapping (another term for EFT) for pulling me out of fear or anxiety, I also use it to elevate my mood and keep me in the energetic alignment I strive to be in.

I also love meditation, deep breathing, and shaking my body to bring down the overstimulation, but don't worry—those aren't the only options. There are countless tools and free resources online at your disposal to try for nervous system regulation (shout out to all the amazing people who provide free tools online). If you're an anxious person, someone who gets overwhelmed easily, or just any person reading this book, I hope you give nervous system regulation tools a try if you haven't before. Don't wait until you're in a heightened state. Practice when you're at your baseline so you can learn what the calming effects feel like in your body and mind. It's about the

---

[3]   https://www.tapwithbrad.com/about, accessed 3-10-2023.

flexibility and adaptability of your body feeling safe, so it's a good idea to start when you're in your usual state to make you a more effective regulator. Understanding nervous system regulation has been like discovering gold. It works, it's proven by research, and it may help change your life like it has changed mine.

Chapter 11

Childhood and Fear are Synonymous

Inner child work is another powerful method to healing, but it can be very traumatizing. My trauma therapy and personal development work was very centered around facing my inner child. You know what's not fun? Inner child work. Is it vital to healing? Absolutely. We all have childhood wounds as an unfortunate factor of life.

Most importantly for me, inner child work allowed me to realize how little me lived in a terrified state at all times. The work involved visiting memories that I had hidden deep in inaccessible places—so many memories of being frozen with fear. First day of being left by my mother at preschool. Getting lost on a preschool field trip and uncontrollably sobbing. Then a group of teenagers approached me asking if I needed help, and I just broke down further in fear. That same year a Great Dane was brought into my preschool for show and tell. When I saw it, I froze in fear and cried. I have countless memories of intense fear that shot through my body like a fiery electrical wire and paralyzed me, feeling like a prisoner in my body where no one would save me, and it kept me frozen. Most people are familiar with fight or flight, but there are two more threat-based responses—freeze and fawn. Freeze is the inability to act or move away from danger (as if you're frozen). Fawn is the action of pleasing to avoid conflict. I have utilized each of the four responses, depending on the perceived threat, but as a young child, I was all about the freeze.

I realized I was always afraid of everything. This came out during EMDR, Somatic Experiencing, craniosacral therapy, talk therapy, and all the other therapies. As a kid, I was afraid of everything, and I had reasons to be. Starting at age three, I fell out of a tree, broke my leg, and spent weeks of preschool in a cast. That was my first, yet least, traumatic experience with being afraid that bad things can happen. All scary things consistently kept me in an acute stress response, which manifested as high anxiety, getting scared easily, crying a ton, muscle tension, blushing, and other not-so-fun aftereffects. I got so worked up I became nauseous and I vomited all the time, in pretty much any public place. If there was a Vomit City, I would have been the first child mayor.

Ultimately, I felt I had no one to help me feel safe. I had no way to tell myself I could relax from the constant bracing for protection, because I thought I needed it. I thought that was the only way to feel safe. I felt alone. I didn't feel anyone could protect me from the dangers of life. I never learned how to process that, and my body still holds on to the bracing at thirty-four years old. It's in a constant state of tension, trying to protect me, and it's now the opposite. Instead of protecting me, it causes me discomfort. My body doesn't understand that differentiation, as it thinks this shields me from even more pain and works so hard to keep me safe.

Negative feedback from childhood sports still haunts me to this day. I have vivid memories of missing basketball shots, the yelling directed at me, and the full-body tension to follow. It wasn't missing a shot in a game; it was screwing up my job for my team and potentially causing us to fail. I put so much pressure on myself to do well that I would ultimately mess up and hate myself for it. My basketball experience taught me that I'm worthless. My support diminished when I wasn't doing well. That led to telling myself that I don't matter unless I play well. I only got positive feedback—or really any feedback at all—if I played perfectly. No wonder I became a perfectionist. I learned at an early age you have no value unless you excel. My brain learned at a young age to mostly operate at a state of high arousal, stress, and anxiety. No chill for this brain over here, and that's pre-TBI.

I was always labeled as a nervous kid, but I didn't know that was rooted in fear. Fear really had its claws in me. And given my history, it's not surprising. I never made the connection that I was nervous to do everything because I didn't feel safe. I didn't feel safe trying new things and failing. I didn't feel safe in different environments. I didn't feel safe playing sports where I wouldn't do well. I was so afraid of the bad things—the unknown. It didn't limit me from doing things; I was just wildly anxious while doing them. I felt nauseous and jittery, with sweaty palms and tension in my cheeks so I couldn't make a normal expression. My heart beat a million miles an hour, and I just sat miserably in my body.

Fear and perfectionism have been closely tied the entirety of my life. I am so hard on myself because I am afraid of being imperfect. I learned the goal was to be perfect even when people say it's not possible. Perfection protected me from criticism and shame. It kept me safe so no one could hurt me, because what could they say to tear me down if I was perfect? So much of my life was built around other people's perceptions of me and protecting myself from the outcomes I expected, even when those outcomes never happened. *If I'm perfect, I can't be yelled at. If I'm perfect, I'm not made fun of. If I'm perfect, I can't be bad.*

I built this perfection monster to the point where everything I did that fell short of perfect created intense shame and guilt. Ironically, the one technique I used to avoid shame and guilt was what brought me the most shame and guilt. And no one was ever as cruel to me as I was to myself. I learned from the best how to knock myself down the hardest as a means of "protecting" myself. On some level, I thought if I shamed myself enough, I wouldn't do shameful or "bad" things. But of course, this never worked and just made me feel even worse. So in essence, I did to myself the very thing I tried avoiding from others. My anxiety shut me down to a point of extreme procrastination and straight-up fear. And that energy had nowhere to go. My thoughts just spun and spun out of control. It makes sense why I loved drinking so much, because it was the only thing that calmed the overwhelm.

Whenever people emphasized the importance of believing in yourself, I'd be like, "Cool. Doesn't do anything for me, but thanks." I used my lack of belief to tear myself down at an extreme level. I proved my lack of self-belief had a powerful effect, and I used that to guide my belief system. Wacky sounding, but my lack of belief in my beliefs is what created my beliefs. Sounds crazy, right? But those fears still resonate with me. I am still afraid of not being perfect. I am afraid of criticism. I am afraid I don't know what I'm doing. But I've realized along this journey you're always going to feel like you have more growing to do.

Thankfully, there are plenty of tools to help with that. Neurofeedback therapy has been a great tool to help rewire my brain to utilize "normal" brain activity and steer me away from fight or flight neural pathways. It works by using electrodes on the scalp to measure brain waves and using auditory or visual cues to create new electrical patterns and, therefore, new neural pathways. It is used for treatment of anxiety (check), trauma (check), attention deficit disorder (check), difficulty sleeping (check), and multiple other conditions. So for me it was a no-brainer (cue the percussive sting for my dad joke). I had read about neurofeedback, but the literature is not as extensive as other therapies, so I was slow to warm up to the idea. But after listening to *The Body Keeps The*

Score by Dr. Bessel van der Kolk, I was sold. Dr. van der Kolk describes how much trauma impacts brain waves and gives examples of patients who, after neurofeedback, saw tremendous decreases in PTSD symptoms.[4]

Neurofeedback requires a lot of therapeutic sessions to stick—and I mean a lot—multiple times a week for months. I knew it was an undertaking, but since my main healing priorities were my brain and trauma, I took the leap and dove in at the end of September 2022. The first step is having a qEEG (quantitative electroencephalography) brain map. This is a baseline test to see how your brain waves measure up to a database of people in your demographic. I'll just go ahead and say it. My brain map was fucked. I was multiple standard deviations off in almost every category of delta, theta, alpha, beta, and high beta. My brain was Trauma City, as I like to call it, full of high beta waves (indicative of anxiety and searching for danger) and beta spindles (which are markers of brain inflammation). Also, my brain was lacking in alpha waves (focused relaxation). There were high theta waves (drowsiness before sleep) in my frontal lobe and prefrontal cortex where they shouldn't be, which show up as brain fog and fatigue. And finally, delta wave activity, which is present during sleep, was seen in my parietal and occipital lobe while I was awake (when it shouldn't happen). My brain was swimming in traumatic, anxious

---

4   Van der Kolk, Bessel. 2014. *The Body Keeps the Score : Brain, Mind, and Body in the Healing of Trauma*. Penguin Books.

brain waves. This was by no means shocking, but I was a little surprised at just how severely "different" my brain was. Not only did it confirm my anxiety was super high, but also that there were many areas I could benefit from neurofeedback.

After a few months, my therapist reviewed the significant improvements in reducing brain waves associated with high anxiety, stress, and restlessness, which were dominant in my brain activity. Surprised those were the dominant ones? Yeah, I wasn't either. But I was relieved by how much they improved. My brain was basically always in fight or flight, which made processing information and recalling words challenging. Those areas were so focused on survival and were straight-up fried from living that way, so processing and word recall got thrown out the window first. It's no wonder I was always going a million miles an hour and worried about the next thing. That's the state in which my brain lived.

I've seen major improvements with neurofeedback, but there is a lofty amount of correction still needed there. Between a life filled with trauma, constant anxiety, and a massive TBI, my brain has a long way to go to be "normal." My brain was in a persistent trauma loop, and I was determined to break free of it. I wasn't going to let fear from childhood shape my brain any longer.

Chapter 12

The Drowncident

For a long time, I thought the single most important childhood trauma I experienced was the drowncident. I can't just call it near drowning because I love a good joke at my own expense, so drowncident it is. I was seven years old. It was February, and my family was spending the day on the eastern shore of Maryland. We were standing on the docks along the Miles River, enjoying the day. My two older sisters, Amy and Sarah, were swinging around the large wooden pilings (support poles) of the pier. Each one was probably double my height and width, but it looked like fun, so I figured I'd try. On my first attempt to wrap my arm around and swing my body over to the other side, I completely misjudged my small size and the fact I had no idea how they were doing it. I went straight into the freezing February water. Fun fact—I didn't know how to swim.

Amy immediately started screaming. I heard my parents running toward her while I hysterically attempted to keep my head above water. I won't say that I was treading water. I would call it more of a moderately successful flail at first. As I kept slipping under, gulping river water into my lungs, I went into fear overdrive. The panic was painful. This sharp heaviness coursed through my body. I'm sure the frozen water was a contributor, but regardless, I was fighting against the pain to keep my head above water and it wasn't working. My eyes were locked on my mom and Sarah taking their shoes off in what appeared like slow motion on the side of the dock. It felt like an eternity. I was barely keeping my mouth above the water level with my thrashing arms. It felt like an eternity. Then my dad jumped in and lifted me to a stranger to help get me out. I remember the feeling of fried nerves throughout my body. I couldn't tell if it was pain from the frozen water or from fear of death.

My mom attempted to dry me off, then soon after, our family got into the car and my dad drove home. I was still in an acute stress response, but got in the car and sat in silence. I desperately needed help navigating those feelings. I needed some serious comfort and assurance that I was safe. My sisters needed that, too—it was scary for all of us. But my parents didn't have the awareness of what we all needed. Most parents don't. Instead, they said nothing, only asking one more time if I was okay when we got home. I said I was, and that was that.

Of course, that wasn't really that. After going through in-depth therapy around the drowncident, I decided to talk about it with my parents on the phone since it was a new revelation in my healing. Twenty years after it had happened, I brought up how I was starting to believe that childhood trauma, particularly the drowncident, may be impacting me now. My mom's immediate response was, "Oh, when you fell out kayaking?" I was puzzled. I forgot about that. Also how was that her first reaction? Of the two, that was monumentally less serious and less damaging. But it brought back those memories, too, which are always fun to relive.

When I was thirteen, I was kayaking on a river in western Maryland with my family immediately after days of torrential downpouring. All the rapids were up a class, so what was intended to be an easy-to-intermediate ride was an intermediate-to-hard ride. I went over a rapid, the kayak rolled, and I went straight into the river. Once I made it to the surface, my kayak was nowhere in sight, and I screamed as my body hit rock after rock. My head bobbed in and out of the river, and I was in full panic mode. Finally, the guide caught up to me and yelled, "Grab on!" I grabbed on to his kayak, and he brought me to shore before going after my kayak. I was hyperventilating, shaking, and unsure of what to do. My mom checked my back for cuts and bruises and said it looked fine, but I felt far from fine. I felt embarrassed for freaking out since I was "fine," and we again got in the car and drove home.

Now, back to the conversation with my parents about the drowncident. We talked about how there wasn't a moment of comfort or processing afterward. I don't remember much of a verbal exchange, only my mom helping to dry my clothes and hair as I tried to stop crying, then walking to the car to leave. I don't blame my parents for that. They did their best with what they knew, which was to focus on survival and getting to safety. They didn't know that comforting me and allowing me to release my emotions would be helpful in that moment. Most people don't have the emotional awareness that not only did *I* need help processing this and calming down, but we all did, too. I think that phone call helped my parents see that.

This is part of the lifelong learning that is the human experience. We do what we think is best in the moment, learn from it, and do differently next time. Having multiple adverse childhood experiences without learning how to cope or express my needs, unfortunately, led to a slew of negative side effects. The National Child Traumatic Stress Network provides many data points that children and adults develop after complex trauma experienced as a kid.[5] These are many of the consequences that directly applied to me:

- Difficulty identifying and expressing emotions (check).
- Respond incorrectly to ordinary stress with extreme response and unnecessary fear (check).
- Chronic stomachaches (check).
- Engage in risky behaviors like substances and exercise habits (check).

---

[5] https://www.nctsn.org/what-is-child-trauma/trauma-types/complex-trauma/effects, accessed 3/11/2023.

- Body dysregulation, including poor awareness to pain or internal sensations, which can lead to injuries with minimal pain (check).
- Shame, low self-worth, guilt (check).
- Using dissociation as a defense mechanism (check).

The following quote from the NCTSN's website struck me right in the soul with its accuracy in my own life: "Having learned that the world is a dangerous place where even loved ones can't be trusted to protect you, children are often vigilant and guarded in their interactions with others and are more likely to perceive situations as stressful or dangerous. While this defensive posture is protective when an individual is under attack, it becomes problematic in situations that do not warrant such intense reactions."[6] Whoa, that resonated deeply with me. I have a full rolodex of memories that were intensely stressful, and my body reacted in a survival response when it wasn't warranted—countless times, in fact. I still experience this, and I'm healing through it. My overwhelming fear response has been the hardest thing for me to clear. It's been so deeply ingrained in my brain and body. And it's unpleasant as hell to rewire and reprocess. But guess what? I'm doing it anyway. Even if it means

---

[6] https://www.nctsn.org/what-is-child-trauma/trauma-types/complex-trauma/effects, accessed 3/11/2023.

bringing up unpleasant memories and having difficult conversations. I'm determined to repair these broken pathways within myself to actually heal, because I know the juice is worth the squeeze.

Chapter 13

My Body Isn't Safe

As rough as it was for my brain, I had an even more difficult time trying to heal my body. I don't just mean my physical body, either. My understanding of my body had to develop. Neurofeedback and many CT scans showed my brain wasn't functioning in a safe zone, but neither was my body, even after months of EMDR, Somatic Experiencing, and other therapies. I still experienced constant tension throughout my body, having sleep issues and high anxiety. I worked through a lot of traumatic events, such as the drowncident, but I had this sinking feeling that there was something deeper. Hypnotherapy, hypnosis guided by a trained therapist, is another evidence-based tool for trauma healing, so I decided to give that a whirl. I found this woman who did online guided hypnotherapy (post-COVID times have really proven anything can be virtual).

The first three sessions went normally, nothing crazy to report. It was my fourth session when things started happening. The focus was on the feeling of fear in my body. As the hypnotherapist took me into a deeper relaxed state, I suddenly felt this piercing sensation in my chest and stomach. It was so sharp I braced and my breathing changed. My heart was pounding. Immediately, visual memories started racing through my brain, and I uncovered the deepest secret of my mind. I was sexually abused as a child.

I started panicking. She asked me to lean into it further, which only put up more resistance. I struggled to even speak. It whipped me back into full consciousness. She kept asking me questions, and I felt my head moving around in confused-like motions. She said that knowledge is power and not to fight it, but everything within my being was fighting it. I was so not ready to face this. I wanted to put these images back in the box they were stored in and set it on fire. Every successful therapist I worked with throughout my life was able to recognize the start of my nervous system spiral and help me tame it. But this person did not. I experienced a full-blown acute stress response, and my nervous system sounded all the alarms. She pushed me to stay in the memory and asked me to relive the experience. I felt panicked. I felt ashamed. I felt betrayed.

But I also felt betrayed by the hypnotherapist. I let my guard down and trusted this person to give me a safe space to deal with trauma, and instead, she left me in the exact opposite state. I could barely look at her at the end of the session. I struggled to find words other than, "I'm okay." She told me she would be there to support me, but I completely lost trust in her. The second after the session ended, I became aware of my trembling hands, and I immediately started bawling. My nervous system went into hyperarousal. My body geared up to fight off danger, but the danger was deep inside of my mind. The memories replayed over and over again on a vicious cycle. I couldn't escape it. I couldn't escape the electrifying fear in my body. I felt the walls closing in. I paced around my living room sobbing, desperately looking for something to help me feel safe, but that place didn't exist. I turned to logical thinking. *How could this have happened? Did this really happen? Did she push me to create memories?* My own body became foreign to me.

After that, it was like a dam broke. More memories came, but in a completely different light than before. I had always retained one memory of my uncle being weird to me. It was Christmas at my grandparents' house, and I was five. They put out a huge buffet spread around their dining room table, and it was my turn to do a lap and fill my plate. My uncle dipped his finger in a cake and dabbed icing on my nose. I turned bright red, which is a way my body responded to unwanted attention, and wiped it off. Then he did it again while maintaining eye contact with no facial expression. I wiped it off again and started to cry. He stopped and walked away, and I took my plate to the kids' table and sat down. I felt uncomfortable and ashamed, but I didn't have the capacity or understanding to vocalize it. I told my parents about this interaction a few years ago. My mom was mortified, and I told her not to worry and that nothing else happened to alleviate her stress. But that's because I didn't remember the sexual abuse. In an attempt to protect me, my brain shielded me from this horrific memory and locked it in a safe place that I couldn't access for twenty-nine years.

The day after hypnotherapy, I had an appointment with my Hakomi therapist. We dove straight into this repressed memory, and the somatic trauma release came pouring out of my body. Oftentimes with somatic therapy, the body starts moving unconsciously and releases pent-up tension from undealt-with trauma, and that's exactly what I experienced that day. All I wanted was for this to not be true. And to my horror, I clearly confirmed it did happen. As the EMDR buzzers alternated vibrating in my hands, more visual and auditory memories came through. The worst of it was the somatic feelings in my body that came up. Sharp fear radiated through my chest like a deep burn. My arms and legs locked up with tension. I started shaking. My eyes darted all over. My therapist encouraged me to not hold back and allow the feelings to take over. Then, something interesting happened. My right arm started swatting at the air guarding me. Then my jaw locked up and I felt my face grimace. My body was reliving fighting my uncle off me. The intensity of the images and feelings grew to an insurmountable level.

That sharp chest sensation was the root of the memory, and I finally unlocked the origin of its meaning. I now remembered an overwhelming amount of minute details about the experience. I can recount such specifics of this memory that I know without a shadow of a doubt that it happened. And the specifics haunt me. But more importantly, the feelings in my body were far too real.

That next week after therapy was an absolute roller coaster. I had a hard time clearing my mind. Distractions with friends helped, but only provided temporary relief. I did a lot of journaling, meditation, and breathwork. It truly set in that I had no safety in my body. I desperately wanted to crawl out of my own skin. I had nothing to help me feel safe. I was violated deep to my core. I was constantly pacing, bursting into tears, and wailing uncontrollably for weeks working through the pain. My whole life, I allowed people to take my power away. I was under the thumb of my ex-husband for eight years. Subpar friends walked all over me because I let them. I received harsh criticism from peers or coaches and took that on as my identity. I accepted when doctors didn't believe me that something was wrong and moved on without resolution. It was a slow chipping away down to the depths of my being.

I never put into perspective the severity of my anxiety or even imagined exploring its origins. The constant fear, pressure, worry, and heightened nervous system were normalized to me, since that was all I knew. I became so excellent at hiding my anxiety by seeking adrenaline through work and fast-paced living and masking persistent nausea through medications. It worked well enough that I thought I was managing it. I was putting Band-Aids on bullet holes left and right, and it worked. Frankly, I thought I had healed it and that high-anxiety Laura was gone. In reality, I found more troubling ways to hide it deep under unhealthy layers. I was giving too much to my career, doing lots of heavy drinking, and relying on an overactive sympathetic nervous system.

Almost every therapist has told me something along the lines of, "I can't believe you've lived like this for so long." Yikes, that's a direct hit.

I asked one therapist, "So most people don't have anxiety like this?"

Looking aghast, with zero hesitation she said, "No." I became so accustomed to my way of living that I couldn't recognize the harm and destruction it caused.

But now it was time to take my power back. I'm not letting this asshole bring me down for what he did to me. I spent so much of my life feeling inferior to those around me. I had resigned to the belief that I wasn't worthy of better. But those beliefs are not me. They are a part of my story that can be released. I am not defined by this moment, and I will no longer let it dictate any part of my path. I have done immense healing, and I will continue to heal my body and mind from the moments that changed the trajectory of my belief system. It's a journey of time and consistent intention to heal, and that is where my belief system is rooted now.

That's why I had to learn my body, even though it was painful. Learning to feel the anxiety, nausea, and discomfort. Knowing was the first step to healing. The hardest nut to crack on this healing journey has been teaching my body how to feel safe. I lived in a constant state of muscle tension and nervous system elevation. My body reacted immediately to stress and anxiety before my thinking brain did.

It's interesting how you don't even realize what your body is carrying. Craniosacral therapy, a type of body-focused therapy, truly revealed just how much trauma my body held. Craniosacral therapy uses light touch to recognize the rhythms and promote movement of cerebrospinal fluid (located in the central nervous system surrounding the brain and spinal cord) in order to facilitate negative energy release from the body. In more basic terms, craniosacral therapy supports self-regulation of the nervous system and releases stored energy from unresolved traumas. I began craniosacral therapy because I had so much unexplained tension in my body at all times that I was unable to identify the root cause. Massages, baths, stretching, and heating pads would temporarily make a dent, but never give long-lasting improvements. That's the beauty of craniosacral therapy. Just like Somatic Experiencing, you don't have to know how or why your body is carrying trauma in order to release it. You just have to follow the therapist's guidance, communicate the feelings that come up in your body, and it'll happen on its own.

The sensations I typically felt were buzzing, concentrated areas that felt cold, rushes of energy through my body like chills, and sudden drops of anxiety into my chest that would paralyze my body. During one of our first sessions, my therapist placed her hands lightly on my thoracic spine, particularly my cement-filled vertebrae. This immediate rush of panic roared through my body. She felt it, too, and pulled back. But clearly my body knew there was something wrong there that it didn't feel safe enough to release in that moment. Since then I've had multiple sessions where the anxiety has taken over my body with sharpness in my chest and tightening in my abdomen. My breath becomes shallow, and my limbs feel immobile. It's so uncomfortable. And it sucks how often I feel this way now that I'm more aware of it. It's been the ultimate learning curve, teaching myself safety in my body. So many years of disconnection resulting from trauma that was meant to protect me required me to relearn how to feel. My body was in a constant state of trying to protect me, and it didn't matter how much I told myself I was safe; my body couldn't let it go.

The more we worked together, the more I recognized just how on edge my body was at all times. I developed more awareness of the constant tension in my jaw, shoulders, abdomen, legs, and, well, just about everywhere. I then became in tune with the persistent chest tightness, drops of anxiety through my abdomen, and other feelings I had tuned out for decades. I never realized how the word feelings describes not just your emotions, but how you *feel* in your body (that was a *duh* moment for me). The sensations driven by my body often dictated the direction of my conscious thoughts, which meant I was always on edge and wound tight without ever knowing why, compounding the effects.

After therapy, I paid more attention to how uncomfortable I felt. And the unfortunate part was how often I felt this discomfort. Anxiety, worry, fear, and stress had overtaken my body, and I was merely along for the ride. A big part of craniosacral therapy is actually feeling your body. Sounds easy, but when you've lived a life riddled with trauma and constant sympathetic nervous system high arousal, you dissociate how your body feels as a protective mechanism. I had to relearn how to feel parts of my body that my brain had shut off. For instance, when I placed my hand on the center of my chest, at first I felt nothing, as if it were a hollow spot. But with more intentional practice, I felt instant panic, immediate fear, and sharp pain-like sensations that descended through the rest of my body to create a widespread feeling of panic. My brain was smart enough to realize, "Hey, this blows to feel, so let's just not anymore. Sound good?" And I stopped feeling sharp anxiety spikes. It's truly remarkable how well a traumatized brain and body adapt as means of protection.

In spite of this fascinating feature, I still felt like I couldn't trust my body. Years of breakdowns, injuries, and health scares, but also frequent blushing and sweating a lot as a kid, contributed to that lack of trust. Once I understood more of what my body had experienced and shielded me from, I opened up to trusting it. It makes me sad to think how much I dissociated from my body. I spent years running it ragged without ever stopping to listen to what the feelings were telling me. Through craniosacral therapy, nervous system regulation, boatloads of self-care, and affirming every day the words, "I am safe," I learned how to listen to what my body is telling me and how to soothe it. Between somatic therapy and craniosacral therapy, I have reached levels of healing I didn't believe were possible, and taken back the feeling of peace that was mine in the first place.

Part 3

How These Traumas Impacted Adult Laura

Chapter 14

Health and Substance Use Don't Mix

Before I decided to heal, I tried to escape my trauma like many adults do, with alcohol and drugs. I didn't think of it that way at first. Ever since I was in college, I made it a priority to optimize my health. I had so many weird physical problems throughout my childhood and teenage years that I felt compelled to make some changes. Thankfully, my undergraduate college and surrounding town had a strong progressive nature, so I was exposed to all kinds of alternative methods. Supplements, herbs, natural products, et cetera were always rotating through my kitchen. I was in pursuit of being healthy, but also mistreating the hell out of my body. I wanted to go a million miles an hour at all times. I didn't enjoy sleeping and had no understanding of what it was like to feel rested. I comprehended the value of sleep, of course, but I never made it a priority. Everything about my life was fast, and the amount of time I set apart for sleep was a pretty narrow window. So to sleep less and still function,

I started looking for alternative methods, namely stimulants. My thought was that sleep isn't productive, so I can caffeinate in a borderline abuser way to counteract the minimal sleep. Then I can have more fun and use my time more effectively.

Throughout college, I lived this fun counterbalance of maintaining an active, nutritious lifestyle while drinking heavily and doing my fair share of stimulants. In many ways, I spent most of my adult life seeking optimal health and escapism at the same time. The outer layers of my onion shell were focused on bettering myself through six days a week at the gym, eating nutritiously, and drinking four cups of coffee to be productive. But the inner bulb was doing anything to escape reality through alcohol, marijuana, and stimulants. I grew fond of caffeine pills (not just coffee), fat burners, Adderall, and cocaine in my twenties. Finding drugs that energized me and increased my productivity? Sign me up. They lit up all the areas in my mind that I thought were the end goal—feeling happy, energized, and able to just keep going and going. My time off was sacred. I had a stressful and demanding job as a NICU nurse, so when I spent time with friends, I wanted energy to keep the fun going all night. I loved it at the time. But what I truly loved even more was alcohol.

My love for alcohol developed in high school. I was playing competitive basketball and field hockey five to seven days a week, attempting to excel in my advanced placement courses, and feeling immense pressure to be successful. And as that pressure for success intensified in college, nursing school, and as a new graduate nurse, the amount of alcohol I drank mirrored that intensity. When I drank, I fully immersed myself in my environment instead of being stuck in my head. In my normal life of overflowing anxiety, alcohol allowed me to bury those thoughts or let them just drift away. I blacked out a lot. I have those good Irish drinking genes in me, and I could hang better than most of my friends, but I also pushed those upper limits. More alcohol equaled more fun. And that makes sense given that adolescents who experienced complex trauma are more likely to seek substances to numb themselves to perceived environmental threats and stressors.

I often blacked out, woke up with some fresh bruises, and did what I could to stave off the nausea to gear back up for more. My friends joked about how much I could drink. I got bombed three to four nights a week. Drinking was one of the only things that consistently made me feel good. Only then could I let go of the incessant voices of my Inner Critic and Inner Hardass. I could put the to-do lists aside. The voice that told me I'm terrible would slowly become muted. The constant need to go a million miles an hour softened. I put a pin in the feelings of panic and high anxiety to be saved for later. And I loved it. I had no intention of stopping. Just like I had no intention of stopping my need for perfection and success in my nursing career. I would have continued this unsustainably fast-beyond-measure lifestyle of work hard, play hard until it killed me. Which it almost did. I truly believe my can't-stop-won't-stop, fast-paced way of living contributed to my health problems.

The TBI is what made me have to stop, which I'm grateful for. For years, I slept less than six hours a day, got 15,000 or more steps at work, partied multiple days a week, and almost never rested. I still drink alcohol, but it is nothing like how I did. And stimulants are now part of my history. I'll have my daily caffeine through espresso or tea, but I don't enjoy that shaky, overstimulated feeling anymore. Now I get anxious after too much caffeine. So not only did I back off on every facet of stress and mistreatment of my body, but that also meant facing how my work truly impacted me.

Chapter 15

Work Can be Traumatic

For nine years, I worked as a nurse in a neonatal intensive care unit (also known as NICU) with the last five years as a charge nurse (the head nurse in charge of the unit). The NICU is a wild place. I'm so grateful that the majority of people have no exposure to the NICU because it's a world that doesn't feel like reality. The unit I worked at was among the top in the state of Colorado. We specialized in what are called micro-preemies, which are premature babies born at twenty-three to twenty-six weeks gestation. Full-term babies are thirty-nine to forty weeks gestation, so that's a lot earlier than expected. Micro-preemies (also known as micros) are babies that are less than two pounds and require enormous intervention to stay alive. Living at more than 5,000 feet above sea level in Colorado, micros have even more stacked against them. They require significant respiratory support to breathe, multiple intravenous lines to provide nutrition, medications to support their blood pressure, specialized monitoring equipment, and frequent blood tests.

When I became a charge nurse, I had been a nurse for three and a half years. That may sound like an appropriate promotion, but in the NICU people worked until they retired. When I became a charge nurse, all the other charges had ten to thirty or more years of experience. I was high achieving, so I pushed myself to take the leap. In 2017, finding a NICU charge nurse job was borderline impossible. It was an opportunity I couldn't pass up. Being a charge nurse was my goal, and even though I didn't feel ready, I knew I needed to take that leap regardless.

The role of a charge nurse is a whole different animal in the NICU. You are responsible for running the unit (literally, in charge of it), making patient assignments for nurses, and shifting around bed spaces to set up for what's to come. You are the resource for policies and placing difficult IVs, and you are the extra hands when an admission comes or when a baby starts to circle the drain. You attend high-risk deliveries and are responsible for resuscitating the baby. You take patient loads when you're short-staffed (which is often). It's a lot of hats, but, damn, it was fun. You become so accustomed to the high-acuity, crazy, barely-keeping-your-head-above-water situations. You get so good at managing the chaos, you have a hard time with the slow nights. I was addicted to the insane pace. When there was a really sick baby, I picked up extra shifts to help, since I knew how much help was required and was already well versed in the baby's history. I definitely chose to be a martyr more often than not. During 2020, I worked extra shifts almost every week because we needed the nurses and had multiple severely sick babies for the entire year. I couldn't be stopped.

My NICU was a large, high-acuity unit (meaning lots of very sick babies) and was almost always filled to maximum capacity. We cared for babies with low survival rates, which produced an understandably stressed environment. NICUs are terrifying places for parents. Not just because their baby is in an intensive care unit, but they are at the mercy of the healthcare team. They can't pick up their baby whenever they want. In fact, many times they can't pick up their baby at all. The tubes, lines, and wires attached to the baby are so vital that the nurses have to maneuver the baby out of the isolette (incubator), manage all of the wires and cords with help from another nurse or respiratory therapist, and then place the baby on their parent's chest while securing all of the lines and tubes to ensure they remain in place. That is often what holding your baby looks like there.

Saying that the NICU is traumatic to parents is an understatement. It completely disrupts everything they imagined their newborn experience to be. They often can't feed their baby because they are too young to eat by mouth and need feeding tubes or IVs for their nutrition. They can't cuddle their baby as long as they want. And when the mother gets discharged and is ready to go home, she doesn't get to take her baby with her. And it is the nurses' job to help them find a place in their baby's care. Nurses encourage parents to give their babies hand hugs to comfort them. They teach parents how to take their baby's temperature in their tiny armpits. Nurses show them how to change the diaper while avoiding the cords attached. They give parents the courage to hold their baby because that is a coveted bonding experience.

I loved taking care of the acutely sick babies. I was really good at it. I loved the challenge and complexity. Some night shifts, I didn't sit down for more than five minutes of my twelve-and-a-half-hour shift. One night, my coworker fed me chips while I intravenously pushed medications with each hand into a baby holding on to life. That's a huge part of nursing. You bust your ass for your patients, and your coworkers do whatever they can to support you. We are all in this traumatic world together, and we show up for each other.

Deliveries can be scary. A baby can come out crying, breathing, and looking great when all the risks are stacked against them, or they can unexpectedly come out lifeless despite zero risk factors. You can prepare and speculate based on the clinical situation, but you never know until the moment a baby comes out, and it can be the most insane adrenaline ride. I absolutely loved deliveries. They were my favorite thing to do. The night shift NICU team gets paged (yes, hospitals still use pagers) to any high-risk delivery, cesarean section, or anytime a baby comes out not looking well. The team consisted of the charge nurse, a respiratory therapist, and two doctors or nurse practitioners, and we would resuscitate the baby. Resuscitate sounds like a lot, but you'd be surprised how often babies come out without a heartbeat and looking lifeless, but with the correct resuscitation steps, they are breathing and crying within minutes. I even became a

Neonatal Resuscitation Program instructor since I loved teaching and helping healthcare providers be more comfortable caring for babies immediately after delivery. I loved deliveries because regardless of the severity of the situation, I stayed calm. I knew I was damn good at neonatal resuscitation, and that was the only area of my life where I wouldn't panic.

Even though I loved it, the pressure still got to me. In 2020, like many people, I did a lot of virtual counseling therapy. There were many horrifying moments to talk about. Near-deaths where you know that baby won't make it through the next shift. Sitting in while parents of a child with a severe brain bleed learn there's a strong probability their child won't be able to walk or talk. Helping to care for a baby requiring emergent body temperature cooling (therapeutic hypothermia) to preserve vital organs and limit brain damage after complications from their delivery. Parents rushing in from home to see us keeping their child alive just for them to say goodbye while they still have a heartbeat. Passing a baby to a parent to hold one last time. Gently stamping footprints of a deceased baby for their parents to remember them. Dressing them in a repurposed wedding dress to take photos for their parents to one day, maybe, look at to remember their child. Yeah, lots of really intense stuff.

During one particular session, I talked about a work shift that was probably the worst I had experienced. My therapist told me to talk her through that shift. Unfortunately, this baby came out of the gates with the odds against him. His lungs kept collapsing and requiring chest tubes to evacuate the air and fluid. He required a ventilator for complete respiratory support since he was not taking any breaths on his own. He was on multiple medications to attempt to keep his heart rate and blood pressure in a viable range. We did chest compressions on him at least six times during my shift. I was the nurse taking care of him that night. When I walked into the shift, he was already in dire straits. The whole gamut of emergent, lifesaving measures were happening already. My first thought was, *Well, fuck, here we go.* I had this knack for shutting off any emotion and just putting my head down to keep babies alive. That was my job. Emotions clog up your thoughts so you can't critically think about what job you need to do. And that night, my job was to keep this baby alive for his parents to be able to see him for the first time.

His parents were young. They didn't understand the gravity of the situation. I encouraged them to touch him and hold his tiny hand, knowing the likelihood of them touching their baby alive again was slim. By the profound strength of the entire care team I worked with that night, we kept this little guy alive as long as we could for his parents to spend time with him. His brain and body were too damaged from the dangerous state of acidity his body lived in for thirteen hours. I gave him a gentle hand hug and wished him no pain, knowing that soon after he would be gone.

The attending physician had "the talk" with his parents around six o'clock in the morning to tell them we'd done everything we could and it was time to let him go. I watched from the window outside the room, motionless with no expression, watching the parents' faces trying to understand what was being told to them. As I left the hospital almost two hours after my shift ended, I had no thoughts. Moments like these were when my mind was the clearest. I drove home in silence. I felt nothing. I was jealous of other nurses who felt more, who always cried with the families.

I was great at caring for families who lost their babies, and I think part of that was my ability to dissociate. I can't tell you how many times I walked into the start of my shift and discovered my assignment was a baby who had just passed and my job was to do post-mortem care and be there for the parents, encouraging them to hold their baby one last time, doing the footprints, handprints, and photos. I could be caring and understanding. My voice softened to a therapeutic tone. I honored the parents' time and gave them space, while feeling comfortable checking in when needed. But I also was so disconnected, and I never broke down. My therapist told me that dissociation was a protective mechanism so I could do my job.

In that session, I remembered why I started dissociating, too. The first death I experienced, I had been a nurse for just under two years. It was the fourth of July weekend in 2015. This baby was septic, which means his body was filled with infection. His little body gained almost double his body weight in fluid because all of his systems were failing. I was standing in the room, with his mother in a recliner chair while surrounded by her husband, the fellow physician, the respiratory therapist, and another nurse. As they disconnected his breathing tube from the ventilator, his mother started bawling. I remember fighting tears as they welled up, and I couldn't fight them anymore. I cried with them. Being a part of this baby's final moments and feeling the life leave his body just broke me. I couldn't collect myself and the emotions took over. As we left the room to allow the family to grieve together, I wiped my tears away and went back out onto the unit.

A few days later, I remember talking to two of my coworkers about what happened. And I'll never forget the ensuing conversation where one of them said you should never cry in front of the family because that's not fair to include yourself in their grieving. *Whoa.* I hadn't thought about it that way. I felt terrible. How could I have been selfish enough to grieve with this family? From that day forward, I chose not to cry—and not just in front of the family, but in general. It felt wrong. Who was I to include myself in these people's pain? I completely sealed up any access to emotions at work. Years later, I realize that's bullshit. I should have cried with them. I should have experienced this with them because I *did* experience this with them. Crying shows them it's okay to cry. This is an unbelievably tragic experience, and emotions don't have to be withheld. Holding back emotions really fucks you up. They grab on and set up shop in your body. Releasing these emotions is not only helpful, but it's important.

Multiple therapists told me my ability to detach emotionally was actually a keen survival skill. But handing a dead baby to their parents and feeling no emotion scared me a little. One thing to note is I'm not a soulless asshole for this. I said some silent respectful thoughts about wishing them no more pain and a better life on the other side. But, man, it sure felt weird watching my coworkers get emotional (rightfully so) and me understanding the sadness, but having no emotions to express. Looking back, this comes as no surprise given my childhood traumas and ability to dissociate. I was built not to feel in traumatic environments like this. Between the disconnection from my body and my baseline resilience for trauma, I was a well-oiled machine in these highly intense, stressful conditions. And after being told that crying in front of family was not fair, I soaked that information up like a sponge and took it on as part of my work identity. But it wasn't healthy. I learned through the last year how important feeling your feelings is, which is part of the reason why I left the NICU in June of 2022.

It's hard to leave behind a career you've poured so much into, though. At a follow-up appointment with my neurology team in early March of 2022, they decided I was ready to return to work. I'm sorry, *what?* They were focused on the fact that from a seizure standpoint, I was ready to go back to work. I had been on anti-seizure medication since the previous December, and I hadn't had another seizure. But I wasn't legally allowed to drive yet. The state of Colorado requires you to be seizure-free for three months, and I was still a few weeks shy of that date. I told the nurse practitioner this, and she said I could start in April then.

The neurology team didn't care about my brain injury symptoms, which were the real problem. It sent me into an anxiety spiral. I knew I wasn't ready, and this was way too soon. I was still experiencing frequent migraines, intense fatigue, and lots of nausea even though all I was doing was going to follow-ups and speech and occupational therapy appointments. I got overstimulated by too much noise, lights, and being around people, which led to migraines, sharp ringing in my ears that hard-stopped my thoughts, and of course, more nausea. I still couldn't do basic math or recall words to speak clear sentences. Yet I was supposed to go back to the mentally and physically demanding job as a NICU charge nurse for twelve and a half hours a day? I was averaging fourteen hours a day of sleep at this point as my brain was still healing. But I didn't know how to properly advocate for myself and tell them no. My injured brain couldn't find the words to express why this wasn't a good idea (or a safe one, for that matter).

I left and had a full-blown panic attack. I called Andrew in a panic. I panicked to my counseling therapist. I panicked to my speech therapist and occupational therapist. Everyone helped calm me down and pushed me to advocate for myself. I knew I couldn't work in the role of a nurse, couldn't handle three shifts per week, and definitely couldn't manage twelve-and-a-half-hour shifts. So I went back to the neurology nurse practitioner and asked to try six-hour shifts twice a week as a NICU nursing assistant, but even that was too much for me.

The month of March was spent doubling down on my speech and occupational therapy. I was going four to five times a week, spending an hour a day doing the exercises they gave me, and pushing myself to stay awake throughout the day. I emotionally prepared with my counseling therapist. I did daily meditations to visualize going back to work. When I went back to work, I wore my rose-colored glasses and earplugs (support aids for TBI survivors to minimize the bright lights and noise) while functioning in the role of a nursing assistant, but it wasn't enough to save me. I just wasn't physically ready. I vomited in trash cans in between baby bassinets, had terrible migraines that forced me to sit silently in a dark room waiting for Tylenol to kick in, and experienced constant trauma triggers from being in a hospital.

I attempted this way of getting through work for months. I slept for sixteen hours after my six-hour shifts and still felt like trash. Sometimes I wouldn't even make it six hours and had to leave after four because I felt terrible. My symptoms weren't improving, and I started slipping back into old-Laura-at-work patterns. Even though I had multiple breaks an hour scheduled during my shifts, if anyone called me needing help, I jumped out of my dark break room and helped, even when I felt like I was dying. I had to be sent home by the charge nurse multiple times because I was so unwell. I was completely overdoing it, and I didn't know how to function any other way in that work environment. I had this epiphany when I realized, *I can't be a NICU charge nurse anymore. Even if I took more time off to heal, I am not able to be healthy in this work environment. I don't take breaks, I run my ass off, I stay late, and I will always put everyone else's needs before myself.* It was a tough realization to get there and was filled with breakdowns, but I knew it was time to let this part of my life go.

My last shift in the NICU was June 8, 2022. It was one of the hardest decisions I ever made. I loved that job so much, and I still do. But I had to prioritize my health and focus on not just healing my brain, but my body and my undealt-with traumas. For the first time in my life, I was fully turning my attention inward and taking control of my life. I focused all of my time on rest, therapies, and healing every aspect of myself. It has been a roller coaster in every way, but I have no regrets, and I have learned so much along the way, one of the most important things being that work can be a source of trauma just like everything else, and sometimes, you have to leave it behind in order to heal from it.

Chapter 16

Too Much Too Fast = Body Dis-Ease

After I went back to work in April, I developed this slow build of hormonal symptoms that were abnormal. I was running on empty every day, even after twelve to fourteen hours of sleep. Emotional mood swings vacillated between irritable anger and overwhelmed sobbing. On top of this fairly severe exhaustion and emotional volatility, I developed acne, weight gain, night sweats, hot flashes, very frizzy hair, and severe fatigue all in a two-month period. Nothing like a good old complete appearance shift to knock the wind out of your sails. Sure, appearance doesn't really matter, and I tell myself I believe that; however, when your life is all kinds of fucked and the only reliable component is that your appearance is unchanged, it really blows. It took me a few months to piece everything together, since I had been so focused on leaving my job and moving in with Andrew. But after encapsulating them into a grouping of symptoms I realized, *Hang on, this isn't normal. Are these side effects of my seizure medication? Are these sequelae from my TBI that have caught up with me?* So I jumped on Dr. Google to see what I could find. No connection with my medication. A gradual sinking feeling came over me. I scheduled appointments with the entire spectrum of my medical providers, who did all the testing they could think of; however, no one could come up with an answer.

Here is a frustrating component of medicine. It's not like the TV show *House* where a group of doctors sit around discussing your symptoms on a whiteboard and break into your home looking for clues. Instead, after the gamut of testing within their specialty is complete, they recommend exploring another route on your own. My situation felt like the Spider-Man pointing at Spider-Man meme where all of my providers were recommending I look into other specialists again for further exploration while none of them provided an answer.

I was so dejected. Nobody knew what to do with me, yet they all agreed, "Yeah, this is concerning."

I reached the end of the line not knowing how to proceed. I thought, *Is this my new normal?* It better not be because, boy, was I tired. Then finally I had my Newton's apple moment and realized, *Is this my body's response to the significant stress, trauma, and change I have put myself through over the last nine months?*

It all made sense. I was in a state of dis-ease where my body was not functioning easily and everything went haywire. The mind-body connection I had been seeking knowledge about was actually being experienced in my body. The state of survival mode I was submerged in created lasting effects on my system, and this was how it was manifesting. It was no surprise my body felt like it was slipping into failure again. Survival mode is an interesting place. Your body becomes addicted to the response, so not only do you seek it, but you feel dis-ease when you're not in the trenches of it. So now that I was out of my job and focusing on healing, my body broke down like an old, junk car.

I was exhausted—physically ill. Nothing could snap me out of it. I was so hell-bent on healing that I didn't realize the backlog of terror I needed to process. Instead of taking time to focus on one major traumatic event, I split my attention between a group of unrelated awful moments like the drowncident, work memories, and memories from my marriage that were in the early stages of processing. So I basically stayed in the heavy, early processing phase of trauma healing. And on top of that, I underwent significant changes in my life. I sold my home in May, moved in with Andrew, and left my career in June. Oh, and let's not forget I was still only six months out from my TBI and brain surgery. I had so many balls in the air I couldn't keep track of what was making me feel what. It was a muddled mix of sadness, overwhelm, anxiety, and strange symptoms that left me feeling broken. I spent months trying to determine what was wrong with me and was making things harder for myself. I fell back into the old Laura patterns of chaos.

Then one morning I had a big mic-drop moment for myself. *Why wasn't I happy?* I was living my dream life in so many ways—amazing partner, beautiful home, and time to focus on my healing, mental health, and fitness. Andrew and I planned a bunch of trips for the fall. Yet I was moping through the day. I wanted to be like, "Hell yeah! Life is awesome!" And I just wasn't there at all. Not even close. My days were fine, but I wasn't happy. I realized when I was talking with my therapist how the point of leaving my job to take the time to heal meant I turned my healing into a job. I was doing different therapies multiple times a week, EMDR, neurofeedback, acupuncture, seeing my chiropractor, and so on, and I watched my time just slip out of my control. I became so obsessed with my healing that I lost sight of the why. I wanted to heal to enjoy the hell out of my life, to find true happiness within myself. But I was self-sabotaging by overwhelming my calendar with tasks. I felt I needed to do all these things to prove to everyone that I was taking full advantage of my time. *Why?*

Here's the thing, no one gives a fuck about you. And I don't mean that people don't care about you, but no one cares about how you spend your time. And if they do, they're probably projecting their own desires or jealousy onto you. I became so wrapped up in the obsession of proving to everyone that I wasn't just a lazy piece of shit sitting at home doing nothing that I made my healing an unenjoyable full-time job.

I morphed my healing journey into a nine-to-five, and I hated it. No wonder. It was all well intentioned. I want to make myself the best healer and the most productive healer! Sensing a theme here? I also was creating more problems for myself. I had been excellent at navigating the storms. So I was creating my own mini-storms because my nervous system was used to it. I felt that coasting with happiness—or neutrality, for that matter—was bad. It's so wild what you can trick yourself into believing based on old patterns. While I wanted more time and to take a step back, I was doing the exact opposite, stepping forward into dis-ease. That was familiar and where I comfortably functioned. I kept adding more and more to my plate by trying new forms of therapies and scheduling multiple therapy appointments in a week, not realizing it was halting my healing. My childhood and adult life were built around being busy, so I didn't know how to make myself not busy. It's funny when you recognize patterns in yourself that you thought you mended, but instead you find other ways to meet those needs.

It's a not-so-fun misconception that once you get the level of success you're after, then you'll be happy. Once I have the money, the home, the life I want, *then* I'll be happy. Unfortunately, that isn't what makes you happy. Here I was living a pretty great day-to-day life and I wasn't happy. *Oh, it's me then, isn't it?* Sure is. I kept waiting for the external things to kick in and amp up my serotonin. This is when the real shift for me set in. I decided to make the choice to be happy. I looked at my day ahead and was grateful. I found joy in everything I was doing through gratitude and reminding myself that it makes me happy. And it worked. I decided to let myself *feel* happy, and that shift allowed me to legitimately *be* happy. Hang on, did people know this? This was a life-changing moment. I had been choosing to only see the darkness instead of the light, but not anymore. It was time to say goodbye to negative Laura, and I was ready.

Chapter 17

Forgiveness is a Bitch, but Necessary (and so are Boundaries)

This newfound happiness meant taking a good look at myself and my relationships with others. Forgiveness is a big piece of healing work, but, man, it is a bitch. In many ways, I was very resentful and spiteful. I could not for the life of me let things go. I had so much resentment toward friends who weren't there for me after my TBI, healthcare providers who treated me poorly, and people from my past who sucked that I couldn't forgive. But one day it clicked when I heard on a podcast the quote originating from Malachy McCourt that states, "Resentment is like taking poison and waiting for the other person to die."[7] Holding on to resentment requires a lot of negative

---

[7] https://www.nytimes.com/1998/07/29/books/lunch-with-malachy-mccourt-rogue-turns-himself-into-saint-blarney-fails-hide.html, accessed 03/11/2023.

energy that builds on itself, and the other person doesn't suffer at all. This was me to a T. I *loved* holding grudges. I learned at an early age that's what you're supposed to do. When someone wrongs you, you resent them and hold that resentment in your core until you die. And it was siphoning my energy and keeping me in a negative state. Fortunately for me, the personal development course I was taking leaned heavily into forgiveness and releasing resentment. It took two main principles to shift me out of Grudge Land—people are doing the best with what they know, and hurt people hurt people. Stay with me here.

The first principle that people are doing their best showed me how people's knowledge can vary wildly. One of the most powerful things I've learned along this healing ride is that our lives are a massive system of human conditioning. We are conditioned by our parents, teachers, advertisements, news, TV, and the list goes on and on. Everything is telling us how to be or what is right, and we morph those beliefs into our way of thinking. The religion you grew up with, political beliefs of your family, the way you saw kids on TV dress and do their hair, and everything else you can imagine can dictate your actions. So if you grew up with abuse in your household, had people who told you you'd never amount to anything, friends who embarrassed you for being unique, or someone who told you that you're unworthy of love, then you're highly likely to take these on as beliefs. And those beliefs impact what you bestow onto others. Don Richard Riso and Russ Hudson spell it out pristinely in their book, *The Wisdom of the Enneagram: The Complete Guide to Psychological and*

Spiritual Growth for the Nine Personality Types. The authors write, "Because no one graduates from childhood without some degree of narcissistic damage, as adults, we have a lot of difficulty being authentic with one another."[8] This is where the second principle comes in that hurt people hurt people. Based on my own childhood trauma experiences, I sought out narcissists as friends and partners, then took the brunt of inauthentic people who stopped at nothing to hurt those around them to better themselves, which resulted from my own desperation for approval.

I have had a life filled with relationships where I was taken advantage of and treated poorly. I have been wronged by a lot of close people in my life, as I'm sure many of us can relate. My modus operandi was to become close with someone, become overly involved in their well-being to try and help, which would ultimately lead to me being taken advantage of and getting extremely hurt in the process. I told myself, "Never again. This is the last time I'm being a good friend and getting screwed over in return." Yet the cycle continued. I wanted to be emotionally supportive to my friends during hard times. I was willing to drop everything and be there, and I did it. I stopped dead in my tracks to meet up with a friend whose boyfriend locked her out of their apartment for the third time to make sure she was okay. Then I waited for her at the bar she requested only for her to no-show

---

[8]   Riso, Don R., and Russ Hudson. 1999. *The Wisdom of the Enneagram: The Complete Guide to Psychological and Spiritual Growth for the Nine Personality Types.* Bantam Books.

and not reply to my messages. I got upset, waited for the meaningless apology, believed it, and moved on. I'd lather, rinse, and repeat this cycle like clockwork. I was a show-up-for-everyone kind of bitch, but never got the same in return.

I'm sure this pattern contributed to my desire (and success) as a nurse, as I stopped at nothing to help. I never said no. It didn't matter if I had plans, was exhausted, or had zero energy to give to someone else, I still showed up. I was essentially throwing myself head first into emotionally abusive intimate relationships that were dominated by gaslighting, which was an accurate description for my relationship with my ex-husband.

Despite having an eight-year relationship, I have blocked out most of my time with my ex-husband. I don't recognize myself when I think back to who I was. That iteration of Laura feels so foreign. I morphed into this person to fit the life he had conditioned me to live. I met my ex-husband in 2009. It was the spring of my junior year of college. My ex-husband was charming as hell at first. He made me feel special when I never did before. He had a rough childhood. He was a classic narcissist. He lured me in with charm, made me feel special, then his controlling behaviors and need to put me down slowly seeped into our relationship. It started a few months in. He threatened that if I loved him I wouldn't talk to other men without him present. I shouldn't give anyone else my attention. If I spoke to any man, it was disrespectful, and I should never do that. And then the yelling started. The locking me out of rooms for being bad. The telling me no one would ever love me. We both had pretty bottomed-out self-worth, and he used that to make me feel inadequate. He gave me the silent treatment if he didn't like who I talked to or I didn't give him enough attention. He screamed at me when we got home about something "wrong" I did until I was shattered and uncontrollably crying. It was this insidious, slow chipping away at my self-esteem and worthiness, which were already horrible to begin with. The beginning was Red Flag City, but I was too naive to see it. But after eight years of emotional terrorizing, I finally reached the point of no more. I was done living this way and used all the courage I had left to leave.

When I thought about my ex-husband, for years it was anger, rage, and, frankly, lots of bad thoughts. But over the last year especially, I've been able to recognize that the way he knew how to survive was manipulation, lies, and doing whatever it took to better his opportunity. That claw-your-way-to-the-top mentality comes from trauma, just like my can't-say-no-do-everything mentality came from trauma. And that's exactly how our relationship played out all the way to the end. It has been no cakewalk, but after tremendous amounts of in-depth work, I've been able to look at our relationship through a different lens. He was doing what he knew to do to survive, and despite all of the screwed-up ways this impacted me, that was how he had been conditioned. It by no means excuses his shitty behavior, but I can now see that it wasn't a reflection of who I was, and the person he made me believe I was wasn't real. I am eternally grateful that

I got out of that relationship and moved on. Don't get me wrong, on many levels I still want to say he can fuck right off and die for what he did to me, but also I'm not giving him my energy. He will no longer siphon my energy and make me feel as bad as he did ever again.

Our relationship was a constant power battle where he was undefeated. Any time I attempted to stand up for myself, the deep cuts spewed out of him. Before I moved into my own apartment, I typed up a letter using direct quotes he said to me about how I was worthless, no one would ever want me, and I was lucky to have him. I didn't have the nervous system regulation or ability to calmly organize my thoughts when being attacked, so a letter it was. He of course tried to regain power and make me feel worthless again, but this time I stood my ground. I told him it was couples therapy or I was gone, and when he started exploding on me, I just grabbed my purse and walked out the door for the first time in my life.

I went to a restaurant by myself and didn't respond to a single one of his messages or calls. It was the first time I truly took my power back, and I was done giving it up. He spent eight years in the driver's seat of our relationship, and it resulted in me losing complete control over myself, my thoughts, and my well-being. But no more. From that moment on, I started putting myself first. He conceded and did couples therapy with me, where I advocated for my feelings, only to be met with his unwillingness to understand. I moved out into my own apartment. I accepted a big promotion at work. When it became clear it was all over, I went to the condo to tell him I was done with our relationship. I told him I took the charge nurse position, and he said verbatim, "Remember when they made you do charge before and you cried?" Thanks for the support, asshole. When I told him I was filing for divorce, he gave me a passive-aggressive, borderline threatening response. "You know, there's no going back from this." He told me to "be prepared" and "get ready" as a scare tactic that didn't land at all. I knew I was the one with the power now, and his words that previously would have been a dagger to the heart were now completely meaningless. He was done stealing power from me.

And the same goes for those friendships that devoured my energy. It took my TBI to finally close the chapter on the last of those friendships. You know what really sucks? Being dismissed by close friends who relentlessly defend their lack of support during the scariest, most fatal point in my life. I thought I had a lot of close friends, people who were truly there for me. I never thought those relationships would deteriorate. But after my brain surgery when I was desperately waiting to hear from those I loved most, I kept waiting. And I continued to wait. I'd think, *Well, they must be busy,* or, *They have so much going on.*

But while I was facing intense, constant pain and relearning which coins added up to a dollar, some of my friends let our relationship fizzle out. I wasn't the fun friend anymore. They never checked in on me. Some of the people I called my best friends never actually reached out after my brain surgery. I was the sole catalyst to conversation starters. I gave them updates because

I thought our relationship warranted that. But once I stopped, I never heard from them again. Or in rare cases, I called them out to say how hurt I was and was met with resistance about how it was my fault. I was the reason they didn't reach out. I wasn't "available." I didn't make it "easy." Yeah, that was a crushing blow. I felt like I was being kicked when I was down—a true reality check. And instead of saying never again to those people, I said, *No more*. No more overextending myself to toxic people. No more letting friends treat me like fuckboys do. I was over letting people who I thought cared about me hurt me and impact my identity. I learned what healthy boundaries were and set them up like an impenetrable stronghold.

And this carries over beautifully to my past lack of boundaries. I don't feel like lack is an appropriate term. It's more like complete nonexistence. Zeroes on repeat for my boundaries. Prior to 2022, I had a limited concept of what that meant. I had let so many people fuck me over because I cared about them. I never put two and two together that loving someone does not excuse asshole behavior. My marriage had a lot of this ideology. Same with my friendships. I cared and overly empathized with others in the hopes I could help, even at my own expense. Well, that was nonsense. I've learned I'm not responsible for making someone not an asshole. Expecting change from people who chew up and spit out those who care about them isn't reality. If you never set your boundaries, people walk all over you, and there's a lot of people ready to take advantage of that.

The big boundary realization happened in therapy (shocker). One day as I strolled into my trauma therapy session, my Hakomi therapist said, "We're going to work on boundaries today." *Uh-oh.* She never had an agenda. Our sessions were centered around what felt most important that day. But clearly this was an established problem that was taking precedent. I sat on the floor in a cross-legged position, and she brought out thin ropes. She told me to create what felt like a comfortable boundary around myself. I made this oblong, bubble shape that was very close to my body with overlapping rope in front of me. She asked why I chose that shape. Truly I didn't know, but it felt natural.

Then she modeled what her boundary looked like and shaped her rope with lots of space around her and explained the comfort this bubble gave her. I struggled to define comfort within my body in a general sense, so not surprising that I messed up the boundary. When she showed that her boundary had a lot of space around her, I thought, *Oh, that must be nice.* I didn't think that was a realistic feeling for me. I thought it had to be suffocating to an almost painful point, which was clearly not the case. But that's what I thought was true for me.

There were multiple steps in this lesson to understand how I felt in my body. How it felt when things (pillows, in this case) came into my boundary. She tossed them at me to challenge how I felt with my set boundaries. It felt uncomfortable. I immediately threw them out of my space. After she tossed a few pillows into my boundary space, I could feel the tightness in my body from an object close in my space without my permission. It felt like someone invading my private space without my permission. I felt anxious, my breath became shallow, and I attempted to navigate these uncomfortable feelings. Then she had me bring the boundary very tight around my body and asked me how I felt. Instant suffocation. My shoulders shot up. I took on a cowering position and felt my muscles tighten. I felt my bubble closing in on me, realizing in this moment that I was now enclosed with my Inner Hardass and Inner Critic. *Not those bitches.* My thoughts got louder, as if they were pressing down on me. I expressed my discomfort with these voices that felt like bullies trying to hurt me.

At this moment, my therapist said, "Ah," and had this expression of realization take over her face. She suggested that I needed inward boundaries for my own thoughts, not just boundaries with others. *Whoa.* That was a big moment. I never realized I could tell the Inner Critic and Inner Hardass to shove it. I always felt they were the hands behind the wheel and I was the passenger. I never realized I could tell them no. After the session, I had this big rewind moment of, *Wait, so you're telling me not only do I need boundaries with other people, but also with myself?*

That tracked. The way I've always talked to myself was super harsh—always *Don't be a lazy piece of shit. You need to get all of these things done today. You can't eat that unless you're going to work out. Didn't you see the scale this morning?* My mean thoughts were supposed to motivate me through pressure, but really, this was a bullying tactic. I learned these patterns to bully myself into doing things. Pressure makes perfect, right? Wrong. Then I was productive purely on the basis of not wanting to hear how my thoughts would beat me down if I didn't. *Oof.* That's a rough one. A tried-and-true move for me was to reframe any thought into pressure because other people would think less of me if I didn't do x, y, and z.

But do people care? Absolutely not. No one cares about you as much as you think. Everyone is caught up in their own thoughts, and you don't resonate with them like you think. But I used the idea that everyone cared about what I was doing all the time as a falsely-seeming external, but truly internal, method of bullying myself. When the pressure of belittling myself wasn't enough to get through, I brought in assumptions about other people's thoughts. That way I had all angles covered. Self-deprecation, threats to myself, and judgment from others was the trifecta of forcing action. So my thoughts were stuck in the shoulds. *You should go for a hike today even if you don't feel like it because you said you would. You should be productive so no one thinks you're lazy. You shouldn't eat that otherwise you'll gain weight. You should do a face mask today because it's been a week and you need self-care, bitch.* (See, I can even turn self-care into a negative. That's a really terrifying skill.)

But really, this wasn't just self-talk; it was my lack of established boundaries with myself. I had zero boundaries with myself, so I just took *all* the shit, just like how my ex-husband and friends made me feel less than. No talking back. No letting it roll off my shoulders. It was always get it done or the voice got louder and more critical. And I sure didn't want that to happen, so I did things to make the Inner Hardass happy, which in turn made me happy, right? Nope. This just made me feel worse. It felt like I had no say in what I did. I never made decisions about what I actually wanted to do. I was afraid of being yelled at by my own thoughts, which stemmed from years of being yelled at for not getting things done as expected. Whether it was parents, coaches, teachers, or other people's parents, adult figures yelling at me hit me on a visceral level. This fear began at such an early age that I can't pinpoint the start. But I have hundreds of memories that led to millions of thoughts that I should do something or else I'm a piece of shit.

I finally had another thunk-to-the-head Isaac Newton moment when I realized my biggest issue with the lack of boundaries was within myself. I just thought boundaries applied to other people. I thought it was that I gave and gave to other people and they took advantage of my caring. I allowed people in my life multiple chances to treat me poorly and countless opportunities to disappoint me. Then I felt bad about myself for allowing them in and giving them my friendship. But in reality, my biggest boundary issue was (and still is) with myself because I didn't know how to say no to my Inner Critic and my Inner Hardass. My Inner Hardass is always saying, *You should do this,* or *You need to do this,* even when it's something as innocent as brain homework from my speech therapist. It was always from a place of bullying myself into doing things, because it worked. And it wasn't just bullying to do things; it was a "this has to be done right *now*."

Stop everything you're doing and do it now. I would have thoughts pop in during meditations, phone calls, workouts, and basically any time, so I would hard-stop and do what the Inner Hardass was telling me. That's the worst area of my boundaries. I allow this Inner Hardass thought pattern to dictate how I live my life and what I do instead of giving myself the opportunity to feel and decide what *I* want to do. See the present tense here? Yes, this is patterning that I'm still clearing. It's a quantum leap of improvement from where I was, but I can recognize there's still a lot of room for growth.

My Hakomi therapist put it very bluntly in a way that stuck. Instead of using all the shoulds, I can change the narrative to *coulds*. I could do this, I could do a face mask, I could work out, I could make this phone call. It's not a has-to-happen kind of thing; it's a choice. Giving myself an opportunity to choose takes away the power of the Inner Hardass and establishes boundaries within my own thoughts. I describe it more as a suggestion box— things I can do, but don't have to. I don't have to do that today, or I don't have to do that ever, but it's something that I could choose to do. That gives me power and takes the weight off my shoulders that I've carried like a permanent backpack my whole life. I'm able to make decisions instead of decisions dictating my life.

I remember going to a doctor's appointment with my mom in third grade for neck pain—not for her neck pain, but for my eight-year-old neck pain. Even at that age, I was carrying the pressures of tasks and perfectionism. I had third-grade neck pain from the weight of that permanent backpack. I perpetually carried this extra weight on my shoulders, and it brought me down and stole my autonomy to make decisions. Now, twenty-plus years later, I had this freedom to make decisions on how to allocate my time, and I could finally remove the backpack, lightening the load so I could make my own choices. It's empowering. It was a stark realization to think that there are people that just live like this. I never had this awareness. This was a part of me that I allowed myself to create. I allowed this takeover. But now, I'm at the point where the backpack is very light, like those adorable mini-backpacks. And it keeps getting smaller as my boundaries within my thoughts get stronger and stronger.

Chapter 18

Time and Distractions = Avoidance

"We must use time as a tool, not a couch." - John. F. Kennedy[9]

Oh baby, that quote spoke to the depths of my soul. My perspective around time has always been disillusioned. I used it as a crutch to avoid dealing with myself while I never felt I had enough time to do anything, always racing to the next task. Even my childhood was so structured with school, homework, and competitive sports starting at an elementary school age that time never felt like a tool. This exploded in my adult life, and everything down to the minute was scheduled. I would live and die by my scheduled task list on my phone. Every waking moment was devoted to doing something, even pre-planned self-care. I guess I can give myself points for

---

[9] John F. Kennedy, Address to the National Association of Manufacturers (New York City, NY, December 6, 1961).

having the wherewithal to prioritize self-care. However, it was always treated as a task to check off the list because I knew it was important. I made it a chore, so it was rarely enjoyable—it was something to check off so I couldn't make myself feel bad for not doing it.

Needless to say, I used time as a crutch to keep me distracted from my own thoughts. I never gave myself a moment to take a breath. I constantly dodged my own mind. And rightfully so, because, as you've learned, my Inner Hardass and Inner Critic are dicks. So I always needed background noise in a subconscious attempt to drown them out, whether it was music, a mindless TV show, or a crowded bar just to have competing noise to drown out my thoughts. I was all in with tactical and audio distractions keeping me from the terror that was my self-bullying thoughts. And that usually translated to minute-by-minute plans. If I happened to have a free moment, I immediately jumped to the task list on my phone to knock something else out. Gotta be productive! Can't let those intrusive thoughts creep in! Go, go, go! Time wasted was an absolute no-no. Ironically, I wasted heaps and heaps of time by obsessively cramming it in my life like this.

It took a major accident for me to even consider time spent healing as time not wasted—like naps. You know what rules? Napping. The TBI was the only thing that could teach me how to appreciate naps. I always thought they were a waste of time. Even when I felt like absolute garbage from the exhaustion of night-shift nursing, I powered through with my stimulant of choice because I equated a lack of being productive with being a piece of shit. I scoffed at people for napping, as if it made me cool. "Naps are the worst." "They just make me feel worse." I said that all the time. More like my brain said, "This is how tired you *actually* are; can you do something about this, please?" But I found a way to dissociate from my body (that good old childhood trauma response), so I easily pushed past it. Avoidance was my way of life in so many aspects. Avoiding feeling anything was the Laura Renner way.

But with the TBI, I had no option but to nap. I never felt exhaustion like that in my life. I'm sure a bulk of that was the trauma-avoidance strategy, but also my brain was *tired*. Rest ranks at the top of the list for healing brains, and my brain didn't let me forget that. I was so beat for the first few months especially. I slept fourteen to sixteen hours a day between nighttime sleep and naps. Also, I was in modified bed-rest mode with no screens, so committing to the nap life was easy. It was bizarre to learn when I stopped scheduling time by the minute, I started feeling better.

But once I reached the point of brain healing that I felt I could "go back to normal," I tried falling back on old Laura no-nap patterns. Those were unpleasant times. I drank twelve shots of espresso a day with a few cups of caffeinated tea splashed in to stay awake to be a functional human. Functional I was not. My exhaustion was amplified by how drained I was by literally everything. I thought I was making it work, but I sure wasn't. I got so frustrated by my exhaustion that my emotional veil thinned and

I just cried. Andrew would say, "Why don't you take a nap?" And then I cried more, seeing that as a sign of defeat. I refused to break that conditioning. Napping was allowed after brain surgery because it was a requirement for recovery. But three months out? Inexcusable. Thanks Inner Critic and Inner Hardass. It took hearing it from my family, friends, therapists, coworkers, medical team, and basically anyone I encountered telling me that napping is okay. I finally succumbed to the realization that napping was part of my new reality.

I still resisted, because I wanted to do something to actively get better, something that distracted me more than lying down and resting. Since my TBI, I've had a slew of emergency department visits. During the Stevens-Johnson syndrome episode, I experienced significant worsening headaches that led me back to the hospital. One of the neurosurgery physicians came in to reassure me that my CT scan that day was improved, and that it's normal for TBI symptoms to oscillate between varying levels for up to a year or even longer. It took months for me to actually hear those words, because I kept thinking, *I'm better, so I should be fine.* I tried fighting through the symptoms, so I could pretend they weren't my reality. But that wasn't my reality.

After about eight months of fighting the need for more sleep than I was giving my body, I finally submitted. And you know what? I wish I did this years ago. Naps rule. I've learned that my body and brain *need* rest, and there are times when I have to put a pin in everything and nap because my body is ready to shut down. Once I actually learned how to listen to my body, I realized how much it was begging me to rest. And I finally listened. I've recognized that rest outside of my night sleep time is crucial for my well-being. Whether it's a two-hour nap or a ten-minute meditation, my body needs me to carve out rest breaks. I'm sure many of us are wired this way, but we've diverted for so long that we no longer recognize the alarm bells, like me. So the moral of this story is prioritize rest. It's not using time as a crutch, but as a tool to heal yourself for the struggles of daily life. For the first time in my life, I'm doing that, and it's been a game changer in every facet of my life.

Naps were the first step to doing the impossible for me—learning how to sit with my thoughts. I did everything possible to avoid sitting with my thoughts because they were uncomfortable as hell. With phones and technology, it's so easy to live in the avoidance pattern and distract yourself. But if you aren't able to take a moment without your phone or other distraction of choice and listen to your thoughts, things aren't going to get better. And no, I don't mean you have to get caught up in worrying, stressful, or depressive thoughts. If a bad thought rolls in, you don't have to get in the boat with it. You can let it pass by. As it jumps to the forefront of your mind, you can say, "No thank you, dreadful thought." Or one of my own personal faves is to say, "Fuck that shit," and move on to something else.

Having the awareness to delve deeper into my day-to-day thoughts, analyze where they're coming from and why they're popping up allowed me to learn how to redirect them away from the bullying, self-loathing ways. I've learned how to get out of the spiral and show my brain that I don't have to get sucked into whatever my thoughts are telling me about myself. I'm able to say, "Fuck that noise. I'm not subscribing to this nonsense." And then the thought passes and I don't spend the entire day perseverating on it to the point of exhaustion. Be forewarned, it's not an easy road, and it's definitely not fun at first. There's no fail-safe method to completely prevent the spiral.

I recently spiraled when I couldn't find my COVID-19 vaccine card the day before I traveled to Japan. I had the babiest of baby meltdowns relative to old Laura ways, but I still subscribed to the spiral. I felt super anxious, and the racing thoughts started swirling through my consciousness. Once I thought, *I'm such a dumbass.* I then went, *Whoa, whoa, no, we are not doing this,* and reminded myself that I don't have to get in the boat with these thoughts. I paused what I was doing, stepped outside onto my balcony to look at the mountains, did some deep breathing, and threw some rage punches into the air. Then I reminded myself I'm a bad bitch and I can do hard things, and then I was fine. It's actually a really miserable process at first. It is not linear. It's required consistent practice teaching myself how to de-escalate and move forward, and I'm still learning. I've been intentionally reprogramming my spirals for about six months now. Each time I push past that agony, it gets easier. Let's be clear, though; it isn't easy. It's extremely hard. Like I said earlier, your brain will continue looping through those go-to neural pathways even if they're bad for your well-being. So the act of breaking them is a tall order, but again, very worth it. Teaching my brain how to sit with my thoughts and not make meaning out of them or to redirect them to something good has been a stretch, but I'm moving the needle forward.

Chapter 19

Setbacks are Part of the Process

It's important to recognize that setbacks occur, because they will come from all kinds of places. You know what re-triggers my trauma? When healthcare providers can't stop and won't stop rambling about your health problems. "Oh my goodness, you've had a lot of bad stuff, huh?" "I would've come in to see you earlier, but it took a really long time to get through your history." "You have quite the complex medical history for someone so healthy!" Cool, guys. Thank you for making me feel even worse about my health problems. People commonly say this because they don't think before they speak or think these statements are somehow relatable, but they really are not. They instead minimize the traumas or make them seem like a burden. So I should feel bad you had to read through my chart to get to know me as a patient? Awesome.

This frustrates me especially because of my experience in the healthcare industry. Here's one thing healthcare providers don't think about. A lot of people have access to my health history, and sure, it's just the people involved in my care. Insert obvious wink here. Actually anyone can look at your history who has a log-in to the medical documenting system, which is virtually any healthcare provider in the hospital. Should they? Absolutely not. That's a huge HIPAA (Health Insurance Portability and Accountability Act) violation and fireable offense. HIPAA is supposed to protect your privacy, but it's really just a threat that requires enforcement. There are some hard stops within medical charting systems, but not always. So this means that my traumatic health history can be viewed by everyone under the sun even though the bulk of my health history doesn't relate to my brain injury. Even further, it's people to whom I'm not actively giving permission who can see every historical iota about me. Yes, that is healthcare.

I choose to go to the same hospital because it's where I've received the majority of my care, so I don't have to relive the trauma of telling these stories over and over again. So being forced to bring them up anyway is retraumatizing. It makes me feel like the progress I've made is actually stagnant, and I'm still stuck in the past because that's all that's being brought up. And in my experience, when healthcare providers read about my health history, they ask me questions to seek information coming from a place of general curiosity, not answers for my current concern. Is my pulmonary embolism relevant to my chief complaint of a severe headache after a TBI and craniotomy? It's not. So don't bring it up. Like I said, I choose to go to the same hospital for ease of history, but every time I walk into that emergency department it sends me into a fiery tailspin. Super heightened nervous system. Fears cycling through my thoughts of what they will ask and will it be triggering. Fear of what the outcome will be because historically my hospital visits were really scary.

I understand the curiosity. Healthcare is an ever-changing world of learning, and I love learning. But when your curiosity triggers traumatic stress responses, that's not okay. It would be helpful to warn a patient ahead of time before launching into unrelated medical history. The number of times I started panicking the second I walked into the emergency department almost perfectly correlates with my number of emergency department visits. I was already super stressed being there, and having people inadvertently add to that stress is really disappointing. Setbacks are to be expected, but if they can be avoided, every effort should be put into doing so.

It's disappointing how many people have zero clue how to speak to humans, yet work in fields where human interactions are frequent. Healthcare is no stranger to this. It's really unfortunate there isn't more human interaction education in healthcare because you can really hurt someone with your unintentional poor choice of words. When I was in the thick of exploring my abnormal hormonal symptoms, I felt an appointment with a gynecologist was warranted, so I called to make an appointment. The hot flashes, night sweats, acne, hair texture changes, and extreme fatigue were getting to me. After the standard introductory questions, the scheduler asked, "And what is the reason for this appointment?"

And I said, "I'm experiencing potential early menopausal symptoms." (Menopause typically starts between forty-five and fifty-five.) She asked my age, and I replied, "Thirty-four."

While actually chuckling, she said, "Well, yeah, that's early!" I instantly felt myself deflate. My first instinct was to chuck my phone out the window, but quickly recognized, no, I actually need this appointment.

She apologized after I said, "Yeah, I know," in the most aggressive way I could muster. But seriously, what in the actual fuck? Thankfully, I was detached enough (hey, look, it has its perks!) to not break down in tears at the thought of my life path being altered (again) by the potential inability to have a baby if I wanted. But I'm sure there are plenty of women who call that office—barely holding it together—attempting to explore conception options. That dumb response would terrorize them so much they wouldn't even show up for their appointment. It's pretty terrible actually, and it comes from not recognizing the trauma in others.

Being trauma informed is actually pretty simple. Don't traumatize the other person. Think before you speak. Think about how the other person is feeling. Why are they calling you? Think about how they might have spent the last twenty minutes shallow breathing and preparing themselves to even make that phone call. Traumatized people can be so good at holding it together, because they are ashamed of making people feel awkward. Read that sentence again, please. Traumatized people will be the sacrificial lamb for their own emotional disturbance so you don't feel like an ass for bringing up something painful, even though that's unfair to them. It happens *all* the time. If I had a nickel for every dumb thing someone has said to me about my traumas, I'd be full-on Scrooge McDuck deep diving into my vault of money.

We all have experienced trauma enough to recognize when someone else is going through something. We know it sucks, big time. Yet we all retraumatize each other by saying things without thinking. Here's an example. Six weeks after I left my nursing career, I received a call around 9:00 a.m. from the disability office that my employer used. She asked me questions to see whether I would qualify for long-term disability. I told her I left my job on my own accord because my injury made it an unhealthy environment for me. She said she understood, but still wanted to go through questions with me to see if I'd qualify (even though I politely declined already). I said yes, not because I wanted to talk, but because I didn't like disappointing people and making them feel the same dejection I felt from my trauma. The initial questions were a little strange and came across as slightly accusatory, as if I was milking the system. But I thought, *Nah, I'm overanalyzing.* Then they pretty quickly escalated.

"Why were you restricted to six hours?"

"Because I had a severe TBI and worked as a neonatal ICU nurse and wasn't sure how my symptoms would be."

"Got it. So you only did six-hour shifts?"

"Yeah, I barely made it through my shifts and had to go home sometimes because I felt so bad."

"Your speech and physical therapy notes sound like you were improving, though. So why couldn't you come back to work?"

"Well, I tried coming back for a few months, and it was so busy and overstimulating that I would have to leave."

"Why did you have to leave?"

Cue the introduction of tears. "I would have severe migraines and have to throw up in a trash can."

"Gotcha, well, can't you do something else?"

"Maybe?" (I struggled to say words at this point because I was crying and barely taking breaths.) "But I was having such a hard time, and it was so traumatizing, I needed to stop."

"Okay. So you could do something outside of the hospital?"

"I DON'T KNOW! I CAN'T RIGHT NOW! I'M TRYING TO FOCUS ON HEALING!"

"Got it. So you can work, just not in the hospital?"

At this point, I was shaking with tears streaming down my face, unable to even think, so I screamed, "I CAN'T TALK ABOUT THIS RIGHT NOW!" and hung up.

I dropped to my knees with my head in my hands, sobbing. She broke me. She kept pushing, and even though I was clearly in distress, it didn't derail her tone or her questions. I felt powerless yet again. I didn't want to be on disability. I was constantly getting calls and voicemails requiring proof through my doctors and therapy notes that I was unable to work. It was demoralizing. Being too traumatized to re-enter the hospital unit I devoted nine years of my life to was heartbreaking. My NICU shared the same vitals monitor as the STICU I stayed in after my brain surgery. Hearing those alarm sounds jarred me in a way I didn't know was possible. It was no longer an option for me to work there. I felt as though they were using my recovery against me, and it burned. I gave my heart and soul to my job, and I was constantly questioned why I couldn't handle being back at work full-time. It was like my Inner Critic all over again, asking me why I couldn't be productive. I get it on some level. Hospitals are fucked right now, especially nursing. Nurses are desperately needed, and it didn't matter that I had a nearly fatal brain bleed and had to learn how to speak full sentences and do math again. They just wanted a body somewhere to help the numbers, even though I already left my job. That was the nail in the coffin. I was no longer willing to be retraumatized constantly. I was done feeling like I was letting my coworkers down by taking the time I needed. No more giving people opportunities to retraumatize me in this way. I was ready to move forward and stop letting people's poor choice of triggering words cut me so deeply.

Part 4

Game-Changing Shifts Within Myself

Chapter 20

Behavioral Conditioning is Bullshit

What other people tell you about yourself can have such a stronghold on who you think you are. You become the narrative. I was told I was anxious and couldn't handle change, so that became my established reality. It was a self-fulfilling prophecy. Once you hear something frequently enough about yourself, you take it on as your truth. I believed I couldn't handle change, so when faced with it, I told myself that I couldn't manage it and freaked out. It felt like I was spinning out of control. I felt so unsafe in my body that my comfort zone of having my nose to the grindstone was the only way to feel some form of safety. So whenever there was any change to my normal state, I lost it.

This followed through to my self-worth. It blows my mind how much my subconscious believed what people told me about myself. Hearing I wasn't worthy by my ex-husband stuck to my core beliefs like superglue. I learned in my early childhood years that what is believed by others about me is equivalent to who I am, so it must be true. I never realized you don't have to believe what people say about you. I was told I wasn't worthy or didn't deserve something so many times throughout my life that it became my truth, and I often said to myself, "I'm not worthy of this." Or if it was something negative, it was, "Of course, this happened. I deserved it." Basically if I was not perfect or subservient, then I didn't deserve a good life. Then, ultimately, the classic belief became, "I'm such a piece of shit."

I took on the bullying I felt from others. So many people made me feel bad for my fear and emotions as a child. And I became that bully to myself through my Inner Hardass and Inner Critic. It was so important for me to fit in as a kid that I took on my perceptions of others' beliefs about me. I not only believed them as a kid, but as an adult. I judged and berated my inner child for her sensitivity, for crying all the time at nothing, only to end up in the NICU, not crying at all and feeling ashamed. Even when I consciously knew my inner child's sensitivity and dysregulated emotions were a direct result of trauma, I still had these judgmental unforgivable feelings. *It's stupid to be so emotional. Why do you have to be so scared all of the time?* I completely took on the words of other kids, adults, and family and used them against myself. That's how deep the wounds of conditioning can run. I had a hard time understanding the way my childhood self manifested fear, emotions, and behaviors because it was so ingrained in me that it was "bad."

That's when the true realization set in. The bulk of our core beliefs are a byproduct of our behavioral conditioning from childhood and beyond. My childhood belief that I'm bad and I need to be afraid of being bad came from being sexually abused and having catastrophic accidents that inconvenienced others. Then throw into the mix the fear of letting my team and parents down in sports or any function that "required" perfectionism, emotionally abusive romantic partners, and toxic friendships. No wonder my core beliefs were atrocious. The multitude of terrible thoughts imposed on me just added more and more layers to my "I'm a piece of shit" story. Once this awareness resonated with my consciousness, I recognized that these beliefs weren't who I was. And with that awareness came the power to release them. I'm not a piece of shit. I'm not bad. I'm not worthless. I'm actually pretty great, and I have rewritten my beliefs about who I am. And now I give very few fucks about what people think. Zero is a bit of a stretch because I still have my moments, but very few is still a huge accomplishment. The cool thing is, you can rewrite your core beliefs, too. Don't let that parent, coach, friend, teacher, or random person on the street who yells some bullshit at you seep into your core beliefs about yourself. You are a badass. And let that roll right off.

Chapter 21

Finding Comfort in the Discomfort

Probably the most instrumental principle I learned in the last year was finding comfort in the discomfort. Stepping out of the boundaries of your comfort zone is a huge accomplishment. That's where the vulnerability lies. The nervousness. The potential embarrassment. But the rewards are the juiciest. No one develops breakthrough ideas sitting in their comfort zone. The quantum leaps in your reality require massive shifts and overcoming big challenges. But really, what's the worst that can happen? You are already where you are right now, so trying to go beyond your comfort zone can only land you in a better place or back to square one, which is your current status. Nowadays, I like to think of my current self as my thermostat. I can stay at a neutral seventy degrees, or I can bump it up to seventy-two and adjust. I can always go back to seventy, but I'll never know if I like seventy-two unless I try it out. This works for money, career, relationships, lifestyle, and literally everything.

My comfort zone used to be my high-speed lifestyle. My previous thermostat was perfectly aligned with my insane workouts, excessive work schedule, solid income level, and party lifestyle. I was too afraid to push beyond that zone. My first big leap out of my comfort zone was when I stopped working. It was a rough adjustment. It tested my beliefs about myself and my trust in my financial future the most. But once I started moving the needle with personal development work, I had the courage to leave my job, sell my home, move in with my boyfriend, Andrew, and focus solely on my healing journey. Now I've been without a job for seven months at the time of writing this, and I've manifested money, opportunity, healing, and complete trust in my path ahead.

Because again, what's the worst that can happen? I go back to being a NICU nurse? Cool, I know how to do that. I love the Napoleon Hill quote that reads, "Your only limitation is the one which you set up in your own mind."[10] That makes me want to kick a door off the hinges and go full steam ahead. If that doesn't resonate with you as much, I hope it at least tips the scale more in that direction. Your trauma doesn't define you. You define you.

There were so many different areas of my life where I was afraid to push outside of my comfort zone. That whole anxiety component can add an extra layer that puts

---

[10]   Hill, Napoleon. 2011. *Outwitting the Devil: The Secret to Freedom and Success.* Edited by Sharon Lechter. Sterling Publishing.

a damper on your perceived ability to push beyond. But exercise is one area I always was able to seek comfort in the discomfort. When it comes to strength training or spin classes, I can be a monster. I love the challenge. I love knowing that my body can handle anything, and I don't back down. And seeing the results is so damn rewarding. But for some reason I couldn't translate this into other areas of my life until I made that connection. It's easy to see why. My healing path has been built on finding my comfort in the discomfort. This is where the real growth happens.

This also meant I had to rewire my neural connections to learn to shake it off instead of panic when things went wrong. That skill of redirecting is clutch. We all have some area where we push beyond our comfort zone, but just haven't recognized it yet. Look a little closer. If you do it in one place, you can do it in another. And think back to that thermostat. The baseline temperature is always going to be there. So is having the courage to step outside of it.

Chapter 22

Be Your Own Advocate

It is an absolute must that you be your own advocate. No one is going to fight for you like you will. This doesn't just mean in healthcare, but in every aspect of life. But let's first talk about it in the context of healthcare. I'm not saying healthcare providers don't have your best interest at heart. I mean, I'm a nurse, and I fought hard for my patients and their families. I gave them so much of myself. However, there are limits to that giving, and you have to be the one to know where they are.

Being a patient taught me this firsthand. Much of my healthcare experience on the patient side has been challenging. I chugged along, desperately seeking answers to my bizarre health status, and everything kept falling through. I had multiple misdiagnoses that forced me to lose trust in my medical teams. Appointments got canceled because I wasn't a priority or they couldn't "accommodate my needs." Doors closed all around me, and I fought to keep them open. I started feeling that no one cared about me. My symptom presentation was complex, yet not life threatening enough to be "cared" about. I lost all faith and believed on a deep level that no one would help me. I needed to fight for myself, but it was so hard when it felt like everyone was against me.

That used to be all I did—fight for myself. But when I was experiencing my lovely health problems in the summer of 2022, the absolute worst of it was the deep exhaustion. I was sleeping the majority of a twenty-four-hour day and was still beat. I relied heavily on caffeine and was still living in a constant state of fog. In my previous iteration as a NICU nurse running a million miles an hour, I slept six to eight hours tops and ran around Energizer bunny style and was fine. But that version of myself felt so far away. I pushed myself to get out of bed every day and make four shots of espresso while leaning full bodyweight onto the counter, hoping I could stay awake to manage the caffeine production process. I forced myself to do my twice-a-week workouts with my trainer that I could barely make it through. I showed up to my spin classes, and despite being gassed out immediately, I suffered through with mediocre output. I imagine the inside of my body was like the engine room in the movie *Titanic* where everyone was drenched in sweat, working their absolute hardest to pick up speed and avoid the iceberg. But I was 100 percent heading toward that iceberg. I backed off my workouts in the hope more rest helped, but it didn't. I needed to find a different way to advocate for myself.

I finally sought help and reached out to every medical provider that would see me. I asked for all the labs, exams, and tests of any kind to figure out what was going on with me. After all my labs were within normal limits (in actuality, all were on the low end of "normal"), I had a conversation with each of my providers who had hit the limit of their scope for what to do with me. "Check with (insert another provider)," "reach out if it gets worse," "maybe reach back out to your primary care doctor?" And that was it.

This is the unfortunate part of healthcare. To clarify, I actually love the providers on my medical team. They are all truly empathetic, intelligent, and clearly ran through the full spectrum of tests for me to get answers. They just couldn't find them. There's an extent to what specialists can do for you outside of their practice. They are masters of detail for their particular specialty, but when you don't fit in that categorically, your provider will suggest another specialty. Not because they aren't smart enough or good enough, but actually the opposite. They are smart and humble enough to recognize their own limitations, so they guide you elsewhere. And since I have never fit into any typical mold, I was left in the dust. But because I'm persistent as hell and have slipped through the medical cracks numerous times, I persisted to get answers. I refused to live like this, and I did not give up.

And that's the problem here. People don't know what direction to go after their healthcare team doesn't know what to do with an atypical presentation, which is fair. It's overwhelming, and many people just give up on ever getting better. I totally get that. But you deserve to get answers and have quality in your life. I get why people give up. It's exhausting, but so is feeling miserable all the time. I thankfully stumbled into a functional medicine practice that operates outside the norm of medicine (which means the bulk of what they do isn't covered by insurance). I realized that I cannot put a price on my health and quality of life and, thankfully, was in a position to take this on. So I went down the rabbit hole of testing, supplements, gut health, and beyond. This bitch is healing, and she doesn't care what it takes to get there. I will forever keep pressing to be my own advocate, and you should, too. You need to. You deserve to advocate for yourself. One more time—you deserve to advocate for yourself. I know I'm worthy of it, and you are, too. Don't ever stop advocating for you. Like I said before, no one is going to fight for you like you will. So don't be afraid to do it.

Chapter 23

Self-Care is Life

Let's talk about self-care. I was a self-proclaimed fiend for self-care ever since becoming a nurse in 2013. I acknowledged how harsh my career was on my body and mind, so my attempt to offset that was through scheduled self-care. I had appointments for acupuncture, facials, massages, talk therapy, and more a few times a month because

1. I knew it was beneficial, and
2. force was the only actionable way for me to do something good for myself.

After leaving my job, I was laser focused on taking care of myself. On top of my regular self-care scheduled programming, I added craniosacral therapy, EMDR, one-on-one stretching, neurofeedback training, and regular functional medicine appointments. Then at home my daily routine included guided meditation, EFT tapping, journaling, an intense skincare routine, and HeartMath deep breathing. My home self-care regimen became a ritual that was a requirement for every single day. If I forgot to do my tapping or deep breathing, I shamed myself for not giving it my all.

Like I mentioned in an earlier chapter, I became so focused on self-care that I turned it into a job. It wasn't about enjoying it or experiencing the benefits. Instead of recognizing that I was actually making myself feel better and I didn't need to rely on the tools, I decided I wasn't capable without them. I learned that not doing my self-care routine actually became a level of self-care. Taking a step back to listen to my intuition and do what feels best in that moment is what self-care is really about. Allowing myself to let go of perfection is self-care. Reframing my need to do every step of my skincare routine is self-care. Letting off the gas during a spin class when I feel depleted is self-care. Forgiving the need to give everything 100 percent all the time is the utmost level of self-care for me, and it took me a very long time to realize this. I was so dissociated from my body that I refused to listen to any of its cues and instead did what my ego told me was right. But, boy, was it far from right. It was such a liberating moment of recognition to acknowledge my body for once and to let it say its piece. It was also a harsh realization that my intended good was actually having the opposite effect. I had warped my view of self-care and did a complete overhaul of my life to truly get the benefits I was seeking. Trauma is tricky like that—even when you're healing from it, it's never a straightforward path.

But now I can look at self-care through the lens that is intended. I take good care of myself. I set up boundaries and say no when I need to. I give myself rest when my body craves it. I pause my regularly scheduled exercise and appointments when my intuition tells me that's best. Getting my ego to go along with this style of living wasn't easy, and I still have my rough days of being hard on myself. But with time, I've been able to shift into true self-care mode, and my body eats that up like candy. I know that when I don't feel *great,* that I will feel *better,* and I believe it. I view the setbacks as necessary pauses on the path toward the life I want. And I use all the glorious tools in my toolbox to keep me aligned with where I want future Laura to go.

What helped me center myself is a catchy mantra I fully endorse—what resists persists. Not feeling safe in my body persisted as body breakdown, injuries, accidents, and feeling like something else was going to go wrong. By not addressing safety and comfort in my body, everything kept getting worse. By not allowing myself to sleep, I only delayed the crash. And a big piece of this was tuning out the fatigue, depleted feelings, drowsiness, digestive issues, and so on that I experienced. My resistance to feeling those feelings made my body get louder. Worse health problems. Worse injuries. The inability to get out of bed. These loud-as-fuck signals were the only way to get through to me that I needed to take better care of myself. I thought I was, but I clearly was not.

Growth in any capacity is a nonlinear process. It's filled with the ups of awareness and inspired action to change, and the downs of what feels like setbacks and hurdles making improvements out of reach. I can personally relate this to pretty much any facet of my life, but especially healing. This healing journey has been a *ride*. So many ups and downs with my health, my brain recovery, healing trauma then opening up new wounds, and my fear and anxiety. So many moments of feeling like I'm failing. That this isn't worth it. That I'll never come out on the other side like I desire. But I'm so undyingly grateful that I never gave up. The amount of growth I've had in the last twelve months exceeded any expectations I ever had for myself. I'm a new bitch, and I'm going to keep on progressing upward. And you want to know a secret? You can, too. You absolutely can. I was at my rock bottom and clawed my way out, dodging boulders left and right. Even though I've experienced plenty of the downs, I can look back on those times as parts of my path that got me here. And I wouldn't trade it. Taking the leap into working on yourself is hard. People don't always understand and unintentionally try to sabotage because they are used to the "old you." But that's no reason to stop. Your thermostat will adjust, and theirs will, too. And if they don't, maybe they aren't meant for your next phase in life, and that's okay. Growth is the power to step up for yourself and release what no longer serves you. Don't let anyone take that away from you.

Chapter 24
Tools That Worked For Me

The key words in this chapter title are "worked for me." Everyone is different. Everyone has experienced a different life, and certain things may resonate better than others. This is not a step-by-step process to healing. This is a choose-your-own-adventure type of setup. The internet has a plethora of free tools to explore, so don't take these as an all-encompassing list. These are my tried-and-true methods that helped me immensely.

1. **Counseling.** I cannot stress enough how important counseling has been throughout my life. Speaking with a therapist with whom you feel comfortable opening up to and who helps you see outside of yourself is unmatched. My therapist knows when to call me on my shit, when to let me cry it out, and how to guide me.

2. **Meditation.** I love meditation. It's taken years for me to be able to lie down for an extended period of time without letting the anxious thoughts and shoulds take control. During

meditation, I can get to full-body relaxation and true centering of my mind. Intuitive ideas come through. Research has shown that meditation reduces stress, improves sleep, decreases blood pressure, and results in countless other benefits.

3. **Deep Breathing.** When I get into a heightened emotional state, the first thing I do is take a deep breath. Shallow breathing is our go-to during times of stress. Deep breathing activates your vagus nerve (the head honcho of the parasympathetic nervous system), lowers your heart rate, and counteracts the fight or flight response. I personally love the HeartMath Inner Balance app for showing the real-time benefits of deep breathing. It does require a heart rate variability clip-on sensor, but the app also includes other helpful guides and tools.

4. **Emotional Freedom Technique/Tapping.** I tap almost every day. It does a great job bringing me out of limiting beliefs when I'm anxious or upset. I also use tapping when I'm in a good place and want an extra kick in the energetic pants. There are tons of free videos online to use as guides and programs to learn more about it.

5. **Somatic Experiencing Therapy.** This was the first type of trauma-specific therapy that opened my eyes to how much my body was storing. The release has been crucial to my healing and bringing safety into my body.

6. **Eye Movement Desensitization and Reprocessing.** EMDR rules. It's just fascinating to experience because it really worked for me. Much like Somatic Experiencing, EMDR bypasses your conscious thoughts to process past traumas and has a lot of research to back it up.

7. **Craniosacral Therapy.** I previously had mixed reviews with craniosacral therapy because I hadn't found the right therapist. But once I did, it resolved deep wounds to my body that allowed me to heal in ways I never knew I needed. Craniosacral therapy is so effective for me because my body is finally being heard—in a safe space, being allowed to feel and be comfortable telling its story so that I can understand.

8. **Exercise.** I used to use exercise as both a healthy and unhealthy behavior. Now that I listen to my body, exercise is especially therapeutic. It improves overall health, boosts mood, reduces anxiety and depression, and can be really fun when you find what type of exercise you like.

9. **Spirituality.** Discovering spirituality has allowed me to feel like I have a purpose. I've never been religious, but finding something to make my life more meaningful pushed me to expand my ways of thinking. My healing journey became something to believe in. Having a deeper connection to my purpose has been a catalyst toward growth and expansion within myself.

10. **Personal Development Courses.** I have taken some baller personal development courses that were the mindset push in the right direction that I needed. There are tons of coaches online that offer individual coaching and courses ranging from an hour masterclass to months of modules and homework. Finding those who not only resonate with your goals, but also address your blind spots, is huge. The investment of a course gives you accountability, too. And there's nothing better than investing in yourself.

11. **Acupuncture.** I've been doing acupuncture for over a decade, but the amount it has helped with my TBI symptoms and trauma healing has been profound. There is much data to show that acupuncture relieves symptoms of PTSD and supports TBI healing. Acupuncture reduces anxiety, depression, pain, and sleep problems.

12. **Neurofeedback.** This has been a great tool to calm the hyper-aroused brain wave activity in my chronically traumatized brain. There are numerous studies to show its benefit for mental health issues and trauma. It significantly helped my sleep and mood, and was paramount in helping to keep me regulated through especially difficult times.

13. **Books.** This is a pretty short list, considering all of the books I've read or listened to on healing. These are the ones that were particularly revolutionary for my healing. *Waking the Tiger* by

Peter Levine, *The Body Keeps the Score* by Bessel van der Kolk, *Happy Days* by Gabrielle Bernstein, *My Stroke of Insight* by Jill Bolte Taylor, *Breaking the Habit of Being Yourself* by Joe Dispenza, and *F*ck Your Feelings* by Ryan Munsey.

Conclusion

It wasn't just my brain injury that led me to my decision to fully heal myself. It was the culmination of five years of significant health problems, and this was the one that finally got my attention. Looking back at how my life has played out allows me to look at the world differently. Sure, I could continue running a million miles an hour, drinking heavily, taking no time to relax or even hear my own thoughts and act on them, and refusing to deal with what's under the surface. But this gave me an almost forced opportunity to face myself. I realized that my thoughts were not healthy. They weren't doing me any favors. In fact, they were detracting from my healing process and heightening my anxiety. Had I continued on this path, the next big health scare probably would have killed me. I mean, seriously, a massive TBI and brain bleed? What's next, universe? That's one hell of a wake-up call. I mean, how wild that it took this extreme of an event to be my hard stop to slow down and make some changes? But guess what? It worked. Here I am. Not dead, healing, and making decisions that are the best for me. Not my job or being the best, or whatever I was doing it for, but actually what's best for *me*. I didn't die because I needed this. And not to say people who die under these circumstances aren't "meant to be here." But this was the lesson that I finally heard, and it required a near-death experience. This was my *oh fuck* moment. And it brought me to my knees in a way that nothing else would have.

Even as I wrap this up, the anniversary reaction of trauma really rang true for me. This is when you experience increased distressing memories and feelings on the anniversary date of a traumatic event. As the one-year anniversary of my TBI and brain surgery occurred, I had an overwhelming sense of flight, panic, and fear, and my emotions pushed up just below the surface, ready to pop off at any point. I had a hard time forming sentences or having clarity with my thoughts and feelings. It was an aggressive amount of fear and overwhelm that possessed my body in a way I hadn't experienced previously. Old Laura patterning would have powered through with nightmarish levels of caffeine and anxiety to do all the tasks and activities that were "needed." But this time around, I gave my body grace and let it call the shots. I respected my feelings. I canceled my commitments. I put this book on hold. I allowed myself to prioritize sleep above all. I spent hours meditating, tapping, doing breathwork, journaling, and other things to regulate. I also allowed the emotions to surface. I am in a space where I believe what's coming is going, and I needed one hell of a release. I'm writing this to show that I am far from perfect when it comes to being "fully healed." I have healed tremendously, but things are going to come up, and I've accepted that. I finally know how to care for myself in a loving way, and that's what I'm doing.

The path to loving yourself is a tough one. You can say it all you want, but to deeply believe it is not an easy task. I am finally at a point where I can love myself in a way I never imagined. I am proud of who I am and the decisions I've made for the first time in my life. I can accept my shadow as a part of me.

The importance of taking responsibility for your own well-being is crucial. You can't expect to feel better physically and emotionally without making an effort to do so. It is by no means an easy path, but a worthwhile one. The more you focus on retraining your mind, the more it molds into that way of living. Avoiding negative thought cycles, pushing yourself to do uncomfortable things, and engaging in positive self-talk are all challenging at first. With time, it gets easier to do it and believe it in your core. Once you have, you'll be able to see the trauma in others, too, and maybe even help them through a similar type of pain that you've experienced.

Writing this book has been instrumental in my healing. I experienced plenty of days where I thought, *I should write today,* and my conscious brain would be like, *Fuck that.* It hasn't been easy to vividly relive these memories, but I have come out of it a different person. It takes a lot of courage to face your traumas. And it's no cakewalk. But the depths of healing I have experienced is something I never would have reached without this process.

My whole purpose in writing this book was to share my story of trauma healing and say, "If I can do it, so can you." Any step in the healing direction is a worthy one. Take it one step at a time. Go easy on yourself. And most importantly, it's okay to say, "No, I'm not fine. Thank you."

Acknowledgments

Thank you to my boyfriend, Andrew, who emotionally supported me through this entire process. You gave me space to write (and heal), but also knew when to check me when I needed to take a step back to focus on my well-being.

To my sister, Amy, for being an ear when I needed it and reliving some of these stories with me. And for helping me feel like I wasn't alone in this process.

To my parents for supporting me in all kinds of ways throughout my life and for putting up with my consistent health scares.

To my ride-or-die friends who have stood by me through all the bullshit, thank you. But especially Ian and Zac, who always dropped everything to be there when I needed them (and usually with a beer), and Ali, who always seemed to understand what I was going through and provided the supportive words I needed.

To my cats, Nina and Bookie, who provided lap support throughout my writing process.

To my mindset mentors, Kathrin, Mikayla, and Andrea, who gave me extra inspiration to change the trajectory of my life for the better. Through your podcasts and courses, I shifted my limiting beliefs and transformed how I look at myself. You gave me the confidence to follow through with this book and my healing process.

To my magical team of therapists who were my guiding light through the storms. You helped me explore the darkest depths of myself and process everything in a space that felt safe.

And finally, thank you for deciding to read my story. I hope it resonated with you, and I thank you for your support. If you enjoyed this book, please consider writing a review. I love hearing what you have to say and truly appreciate your feedback. Thank you!

www.ingramcontent.com/pod-product-compliance
Lightning Source LLC
Chambersburg PA
CBHW020246130626
46549CB00005B/2082